Private Collection 2

Private Collection 2

recipes from the Junior League of Palo Alto

edited by Bonnie Stewart Mickelson

illustrated by Linda Newberry

The Junior League of Palo Alto, Inc.
555 Ravenswood Avenue, Menlo Park
California 94025
©1984 by The Junior League
of Palo Alto, Inc.
Printed in the United States of America
First Published in September, 1984
Second Impression December, 1984

The purpose of the Junior League is exclusively educational and
charitable and is to promote voluntarism, to develop the potential
of its members for voluntary participation in community affairs, and
to demonstrate the effectiveness of the volunteer.

THE COMMITTEE

Chairman
Patricia Ireland Fuller

Editor
Bonnie Stewart Mickelson

Recipe Coordinator
Mary Davis Sweeney

Testing Coordinator
Catherine Kinney Salera

Sarah McCall Grant
Joan Emery Hagey
Judith Rockwell Humphreys
Janet King Littlefield
Sharon Zweig Meresman

Recipe Testers and Readers

Alice Charleston Anderson
Suzanne Lafferty Beim
Pamela Flebbe Brandin
Betsy Lovell Hawley
Kristin Ekstrom Klint

Mimi Platt Menard
Phoebe Allen Olcott
Marilyn Moore Pratt
Jamie Bingham Sidells
Chris Larson Terborgh

We are very proud to bring you another *private collection* of our favorite recipes. As with our first *Private Collection*, these have been tested with great care, then selected for discerning cooks and hostesses, with today's modes of living in mind. We hope you will treasure them as we have.

The Committee

To our dear friends,
whose encouragement,
generosity, and warm support
have inspired
another "private collection."

A beautiful summer refresher.

Yield
3 quarts

4 tea bags
12 large, fresh mint leaves
3 cups boiling water
1 cup orange juice
¼ cup lemon juice
1 cup sugar
6 cups water
Sprigs of mint
Orange slices

Preparation
5 minutes

Cool

Place tea bags and mint leaves in a 3-quart pitcher. Add 3 cups boiling water and steep until cool. Discard tea bags and mint leaves.

Add orange and lemon juices, sugar, and 6 cups of water to tea mixture, stirring until sugar is dissolved. Serve over ice and garnish with mint sprigs and orange slices.

2 GINGER TEA

Yield
6 cups

Preparation
5 minutes

Beloved by all who joined his cooking classes, Mr. Loo, and his special touches, can be detected throughout this book. As one of our committee noted, he was "our Renaissance man from China," and no cooking lesson was complete without an extraordinary tale of his early years in the Orient. GINGER TEA is a delicious testimony to his remarkable, long life.

4 ¼-inch thick slices ginger root
¼ cup light brown sugar
6 cups boiling water

Bruise ginger slices with the flat side of a large knife blade. Place in a 6-cup teapot with brown sugar and boiling water. Steep 5 minutes.

No! We didn't omit anything, and those sipping it will vow that it is real tea!

3 CINNAMON STICKS

Yield
2 to 3 dozen

Preparation
20 minutes

. . . seem just right with GINGER TEA, and they keep nicely.

1 cup sugar
¼ cup ground cinnamon
1 loaf white bread, unsliced
1 cup butter, melted

Preheat oven to 400°.

Combine sugar and cinnamon. Trim crusts from bread. Cut bread into 1-inch thick slices. Cut each slice into 1 x 4-inch sticks (about 4 per slice). Dip in melted butter and roll in cinnamon-sugar. Place on foil-lined cookie sheet. Bake 15 minutes, or until crisp and slightly brown.

The surprise is not only how wonderful these are, but the variety of occasions they can bless. Prepare open-faced for lovely luncheons, teatime, champagne receptions. . . .

Yield
(see below)

Preparation
25 minutes

1 cup diced, cooked chicken
  (about 1 whole breast)
½ cup finely chopped dates
¼ cup chopped hazelnuts (filberts)
¼ cup crumbled, crisp bacon (about 4 strips)
½ cup mayonnaise
Salt (optional)
12 thin slices white bread, buttered

Chicken should be diced in ¼-inch cubes. If hazelnuts still have their skins, place in a 350° oven for 10–15 minutes, until skins split. When cool, rub between hands or a rough towel to remove skins.

Combine all ingredients (except bread), adding salt if necessary. Spread on buttered bread slices, then trim crusts. Cut into desired number of triangles: 2 per slice for luncheon, 4 per slice for teatime, and 6 or 8 per slice for canapes.

Absolutely superb with CALIFORNIA ORANGE SOUP or CARROT VICHYSSOISE.

5 WATERCRESS SANDWICHES

Yield 16

*Serves
8 to 12*

*Preparation
30 minutes*

The queen of dainty tea sandwiches, this recipe of English origin has been passed down from generation to generation. It's a lovely touch for luncheon plates and delicate soups.

1 1-pound loaf of thinly-sliced white bread
6 tablespoons butter, softened
⅓ cup finely chopped watercress sprigs
1 teaspoon grated onion
½ teaspoon Worcestershire sauce
¼ teaspoon salt
Freshly ground pepper
Watercress sprigs

Trim crusts from bread slices, then roll thin with a rolling pin. Combine remaining ingredients, except watercress sprigs. Generously spread on bread slices and roll up.

At this point, the sandwiches may be covered with waxed paper, a damp towel, and then plastic wrap, and refrigerated up to 24 hours; but they should be served at room temperature.

Serve whole or cut in half for a daintier appearance. Tuck sprigs of watercress in ends.

STUFFED CHERRY TOMATOES 6

How lucky you are! Both of these are so good that there was no way to choose just one for our book.

Hollow out 36 cherry tomatoes and turn upside down to drain on paper towels. If you wish them to stand up nicely when served, cut thin slices from the bottoms.

BACON FILLING

1 ½ pounds bacon, chopped
8 green onions, finely chopped
⅓ cup mayonnaise

Fry bacon until crisp and drain well. Mix with green onions and mayonnaise. Stuff tomatoes and chill.

CRAB CREAM FILLING

1 cup shredded crab meat
¼ cup fresh lime juice
3 ounces cream cheese, softened
¼ cup cream
2 tablespoons mayonnaise
1 tablespoon minced onion
½ teaspoon minced garlic
1 teaspoon dried dill weed
1 teaspoon Worcestershire sauce
2 drops Tabasco sauce
Salt to taste

Marinate crab meat in lime juice for 1 hour. Drain well. Combine cream cheese, cream, and mayonnaise until smooth. Mix together with drained crab meat and remaining ingredients. Fill tomatoes and chill.

Yield 36

*Preparation
45 minutes*

Chill

Yield 36

*Marinate
1 hour*

*Preparation
45 minutes*

Chill

7 ASPARAGUS ROLLS

Yield 75

*Preparation
30 minutes*

Freeze

*Baking
15 minutes*

Both the appearance and the taste are beautiful . . . truly a superb hors d'œuvre.

> 25 fresh asparagus spears
> Salt to taste
> 25 thin slices white bread
> 8 ounces cream cheese, softened
> 3 ounces blue cheese, softened
> 1 egg
> ¾ pound butter, melted

In a large skillet, bring enough water to boil to barely cover asparagus. Trim spears to same length as bread slices and place in skillet. Sprinkle with salt and partially cover with a lid. Boil gently until lower parts of stalks are *barely* fork-tender; about 3–5 minutes, depending on age of asparagus. Drain immediately and rinse in cold water until cooking process has ended.

Remove crusts from bread and flatten slices with a rolling pin. Combine cheeses and egg with an electric beater. Spread mixture evenly over bread slices. Place an asparagus spear on each one and roll up. Dip in melted butter to coat all sides. Place on a cookie sheet and freeze until ready to bake.

Preheat oven to 400°. Cut frozen rolls into thirds and bake, still frozen, for 15 minutes or until lightly browned. Serve immediately.

These are a melt-in-your-mouth, perennial favorite.

2½ cups flour
1 cup butter, softened
1 cup sour cream
Seasoned salt to taste
3 cups (12 ounces) shredded sharp cheddar cheese
Paprika

Yield
4 dozen

Preparation
15 minutes

Chill

Baking
25–30
minutes

In a bowl, combine flour, butter, and sour cream until well-mixed. Divide into 4 equal parts, wrapping each in plastic film. Refrigerate until firm.

Using a floured pastry cloth and rolling-pin cover (or place dough between 2 sheets of waxed paper), roll portions out into 6 x 12-inch rectangles. Sprinkle each with seasoned salt and ¾ cup of shredded cheese. Starting with the long side toward you, roll up each one in jelly-roll fashion. Seal edges and ends by pressing together. Wrap in plastic film and refrigerate until baking time.

Preheat oven to 350°. Using a sharp knife, cut rolls, seam-side down, into 1-inch thick slices and place on ungreased cookie sheets (about 12–15 per sheet). Sprinkle with paprika. Bake 25–30 minutes, until golden brown. Serve while still warm.

Note: The unsliced rolls freeze beautifully for handy, last-minute appetizers.

9 MUSHROOM CROUSTADES

Yield
2 dozen

Preparation
45 minutes

Freeze
(optional)

Baking
10 minutes

This is one of those recipes that has been closely guarded by caterers and proudly demonstrated by cooking instructors for years. It is a must in your collection. The tartlets can be made in quantity and frozen.

24 thin slices white bread
2 tablespoons butter, softened

Preheat oven to 400°. Cut a 3-inch round from each bread slice. Brush insides of 2 miniature muffin tins generously with butter. Gently fit bread rounds into each mold to form a cup. Bake 10 minutes or until lightly browned. Cool.

3 tablespoons minced shallots
¼ cup butter
½ pound fresh mushrooms, finely chopped
2 tablespoons flour
1 cup heavy cream
1½ tablespoons minced chives
1 tablespoon minced parsley
½ teaspoon lemon juice
½ teaspoon salt
⅛ teaspoon cayenne pepper

In a heavy skillet, sauté shallots in butter for 1 minute. Stir in mushrooms and simmer, uncovered, until all liquid has evaporated; about 10 minutes.

Remove from heat and stir flour into mushrooms. Pour cream over and return to heat. Stirring constantly, bring to a boil and cook another minute or so while mixture becomes very thick. Remove from heat and stir in remaining ingredients. Let cool, then cover and refrigerate.

At this point, you may spoon the mushroom mixture into the toast shells and freeze in their tins. Once frozen, remove to plastic bags for easier freezer storage.

2 tablespoons freshly grated Parmesan cheese
2 teaspoons minced parsley
Butter

Thaw croustades completely before baking. Preheat oven to 350°. Sprinkle each one with Parmesan cheese and parsley. Dot with specks of butter and arrange on an ungreased baking sheet. Bake 10 minutes; then, if you wish, pop under broiler for a quick browning. Serve immediately.

GULLIXSON CRAB 10

This is a smashing hors d'oeuvre for those of us who never seem to have enough time in the day to prepare such good things.

Serves 8 to 10

Preparation 10 minutes

1 small onion (or 1 bunch green onions), chopped
12 ounces cream cheese, softened
2 tablespoons butter, softened
1 tablespoon Worcestershire sauce
1 tablespoon lemon juice
6 ounces seafood sauce
1–1½ tablespoons horseradish
½ pound seafood (crab meat or coarsely chopped shrimp)
Watercress or parsley

Combine onion, cream cheese, butter, Worcestershire sauce, and lemon juice. (A food processor does this beautifully.) Spread into a 1-inch thick circle or square on an attractive platter. Combine seafood sauce and horseradish, and pour over cheese mixture. Top with seafood and garnish with watercress or parsley. Serve with thin crackers or melbas.

11 SHRIMP BREAD

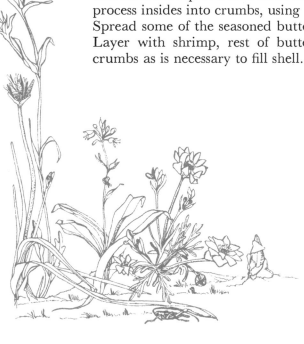

Serves 12

*Preparation
25 minutes*

*Baking
25–30
minutes*

Elegant picnics, dinner parties, or cocktail buffets . . . no matter where, this unusual appetizer will bring many compliments. As a first course, consider serving on small plates in the living room for your guests to enjoy while you attend to such nice things as candle-lighting.

½ cup finely chopped parsley
3 large cloves garlic, minced
2 tablespoons finely chopped shallots
2 tablespoons ground blanched almonds
1 tablespoon Pernod aperitif
1½ teaspoons salt
1 teaspoon white pepper
½ pound unsalted butter, softened

Preheat oven to 400°. Combine above ingredients. (If you have a food processor, the parsley, garlic, shallots, and almonds may be chopped together, then added to the rest.)

1 loaf French bread (about 4½ x 14 inches)
1¼ pounds large bay shrimp (or small gulf shrimp), cooked
½ cup dry white wine

Cut lid from top of bread and reserve. Hollow out bread and process insides into crumbs, using a blender or food processor. Spread some of the seasoned butter in bottom of bread shell. Layer with shrimp, rest of butter, and as much of bread crumbs as is necessary to fill shell. Drizzle wine over top.

Place bread on a foil-lined cookie sheet, without its lid. Bake 15 minutes. Cover with lid and bake another 10 minutes, or until bread is heated through and butter has melted. Slice into 12 servings.

This may be served hot or cold, and is every bit as good the next day, reheated.

Note: The seasoned butter is luscious on broiled fish.

CEVICHE **12**

Grand for cocktail or tailgate parties, picnics, or as a first course to dinner parties.

Serves 6

Preparation 10 minutes

Marinate 2 days

      1 pound firm, white fish (halibut, sea bass, ling cod)
      ¼ cup fresh lime juice
      2 tomatoes, peeled, seeded, and chopped
      ½ cup chopped red onion (or green)
      2 garlic cloves, minced
      Salt to taste
      3–4 sprigs cilantro

Cut fish into ¾-inch cubes. Mix with remaining ingredients, including cilantro. Refrigerate in a covered container for 2 days, stirring twice each day.

Serve on beds of butter lettuce with sprigs of cilantro as a first course, or with crackers for hors d'oeuvres.

13 TWO-DAY FILLET of BEEF

Serves 12

*Preparation
25 minutes*

*Marinate
24–40 hours*

Your butcher may not love you, but your guests will! A perfect addition to cocktail buffets and tailgate parties, serve with baguettes of French bread.

Since it is vital that the beef be sliced paper-thin, place your order with the butcher several days in advance so that he will have time to freeze the meat (trimmed of *all* fat) for easier slicing.

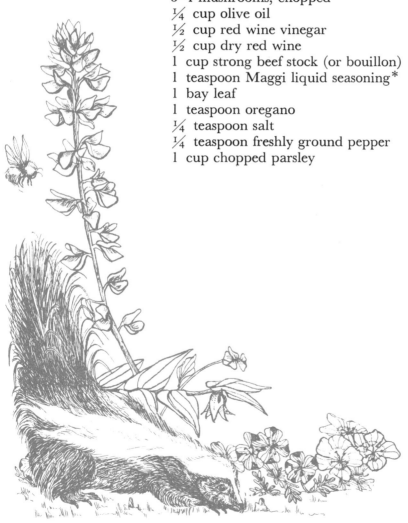

2 pounds lean fillet of beef
1 onion, finely chopped
2 cloves garlic, minced
3–4 mushrooms, chopped
¼ cup olive oil
½ cup red wine vinegar
½ cup dry red wine
1 cup strong beef stock (or bouillon)
1 teaspoon Maggi liquid seasoning*
1 bay leaf
1 teaspoon oregano
¼ teaspoon salt
¼ teaspoon freshly ground pepper
1 cup chopped parsley

The marinade acts as the cooking process. Marinate the beef (according to the following instructions) in the refrigerator for 24 hours for rare, 40 hours for medium.

Sauté onion, garlic, and mushrooms in olive oil until soft. Add vinegar and let boil until reduced by half. Add remaining ingredients, except parsley, and simmer 5 minutes.

In a large, heat-proof dish, arrange half of the beef in one layer; cover with parsley and top with remaining beef, in one layer. Pour boiling-hot marinade over all and cover tightly with plastic film or foil. Refrigerate for desired length of time.

At least 1 hour before serving, remove meat from refrigerator to reach room temperature.

Arrange beef slices attractively on serving platter and pour some of the marinade over top. Supply a basket of small, lightly buttered, bread slices. It's wonderful! If you have our first *Private Collection*, serve with MAISON JAUSSAUD'S BEANS and cornichons for a tailgate treat.

*You may substitute any strong steak sauce for the Maggi seasoning, but double the amount.

14 CARROT VICHYSSOISE

Serves
6 to 10

Preparation
20 minutes

Chill

Here's the perfect soup to spark your early-spring luncheon or dinner party. As a companion to PASTA SALAD, it's gorgeous!

4½ cups diced potatoes
3½ cups diced carrots
2 cups chopped leeks
6 cups chicken broth
2 teaspoons instant chicken bouillon
2 cups light cream
½ teaspoon salt
¼ teaspoon white pepper
3 tablespoons grated raw carrot
Dill weed or minced chives

Place vegetables, chicken broth, and instant bouillon in large saucepan. Bring to a boil and simmer, covered, about 10 minutes, or until vegetables are tender.

Puree vegetables in an electric blender until very smooth. Place in a bowl, adding cream, salt, and white pepper. (The zippy touch of white pepper is very important to this soup.) Chill.

Check seasoning before serving in chilled bowls. Sprinkle grated carrot and dill weed or minced chives on top.

Avocados and limes and California sunshine . . . this soup is testimony of how well they suit each other.

Serves 8

Preparation 10 minutes

Chill

    6 ripe avocados
    5 cups chicken broth
    2 cups light cream
    3–4 tablespoons fresh lime juice
    Dash or 2 of Tabasco sauce
    Pinch of cayenne pepper
    Salt and pepper to taste
    Thin slices of lime
    Cilantro sprigs

Puree avocados with chicken broth in a food processor or blender. Combine with remaining ingredients, blending well with a whisk. Chill.

Serve in ice-cold soup cups, garnishing each with a paper-thin slice of lime and a sprig of cilantro (Chinese parsley).

16 CALIFORNIA ORANGE SOUP

Serves 10 to 12

Preparation 25 minutes

Chill

Pretty, refreshing . . . a most unusual soup for a summer luncheon or brunch. On a hot day, serve with WATERCRESS SANDWICHES as a first or main course, or feature in frosted wine goblets with MOLASSES CRISPS as an evening dessert.

4½ cups fresh orange juice
1 cup fresh lemon juice
2 tablespoons sugar
2 tablespoons quick-cooking tapioca
Dash of salt
2 cinnamon sticks
4 cups sliced, fresh peaches
1 cup sugar
¼ cup flour
¼ teaspoon cinnamon
1½ cups orange sections
1 banana, sliced
¼ cup Cointreau liqueur (optional)
Sour cream (optional)
½ pint fresh raspberries (optional)

Combine the orange and lemon juices, sugar, tapioca, and salt in a large saucepan. Let stand 5 minutes. Add cinnamon sticks and bring to a boil over medium heat. Let simmer, uncovered, for 5 minutes, stirring occasionally.

Combine sliced peaches, sugar, flour, and cinnamon. Add to pan and simmer another 5 minutes, stirring from time to time. Remove from heat and cool.

Cut orange sections into bite-sized pieces, removing any membrane. Add to cooled soup with sliced banana and Cointreau. Remove cinnamon sticks and chill well.

To serve, ladle into chilled soup cups or goblets. If you wish, garnish each with a tablespoon of sour cream and a few fresh raspberries.

Note: If preparing a day in advance, do not add banana slices until several hours before serving.

My, but this is good! The lemon juice and ground coriander are the secrets. Serve hot or cold.

Serves 6

*Preparation
25 minutes*

2½ pounds fresh asparagus
   (or 2 10-ounce packages frozen)
1 small onion, chopped
¼ cup minced parsley
1½ teaspoons ground coriander
3 tablespoons butter
1 tablespoon flour
3 cups chicken broth
1 cup heavy cream
2 tablespoons lemon juice
Salt and white pepper

Cook asparagus until tender. Rinse immediately in cold water and drain. Cut 1-inch tips from stalks and reserve. Cut the stalks into 1-inch pieces.

In a large saucepan, sauté onion, parsley, and coriander in butter until vegetables are softened. Sprinkle in flour and cook for 2–3 minutes, stirring with a whisk. Remove from heat and stir in chicken broth. Return to heat and simmer, stirring occasionally, for 5 minutes.

Add cut asparagus stalks to broth mixture. Puree in blender, in batches, until smooth. Pour into a large, heavy saucepan and stir in cream and reserved asparagus tips. (If you wish, save 6 tips for garnishing.) Over moderate heat, reheat soup but do not boil. Stir in lemon juice, then salt and white pepper to taste.

SUGGESTIONS FOR GARNISHING: buttered toast rounds sprinkled with grated Parmesan cheese and topped with asparagus tips, thin lemon slices dusted with minced parsley, or dollops of sour cream sprinkled with chopped chives.

18 SWISS BROCCOLI SOUP

Serves
6 to 8

Preparation
30 minutes

A glorious way to use a glorious vegetable.

2½ pounds broccoli
1 cup chopped leeks or green onions
4 tablespoons butter
4 tablespoons flour
4 cups rich chicken stock
1 cup light cream
1 cup shredded Swiss cheese
⅛ teaspoon nutmeg
Salt and freshly ground pepper

Cut enough 1-inch florets from broccoli to measure 2 cups. Cut rest of broccoli into 1-inch pieces. Cook florets and broccoli pieces, separately, in lightly salted water; until *just* tender. (Florets will be done first.) Immediately rinse in cold water to chill completely. Drain. Set florets aside until serving time.

In a large saucepan, sauté leeks in butter until tender; about 3–4 minutes. Sprinkle in flour and cook for a minute or so, stirring with a whisk. Remove from heat and stir in chicken stock. Return to heat and simmer 5 minutes, stirring occasionally.

Add broccoli pieces (not florets) to chicken stock and puree in an electric blender, in batches, until smooth.

Shortly before serving, blend in cream and cheese. Simmer gently until cheese melts. Add nutmeg, and salt and pepper to taste. Add reserved broccoli florets to heat through. Serve immediately.

The appeal is in the simplicity . . . the incomparable flavor of fresh tomatoes is allowed to be center-stage.

Serves
6 to 8

3 tablespoons butter
1 medium onion, sliced
1 clove garlic, minced
5 large, well-ripened tomatoes*
1 tablespoon chopped fresh basil (optional)
¼ teaspoon dry mustard
¼ teaspoon salt
⅛ teaspoon freshly ground pepper
¼ cup tomato paste
¼ cup flour
2 cups chicken broth
1–2 cups light cream
2–4 tablespoons sherry (optional)

Preparation
20 minutes

In a deep saucepan, melt butter and sauté onion and garlic until golden. Slice tomatoes and add with dry mustard, salt, and pepper. Simmer, uncovered, 8–10 minutes.

Stir in tomato paste. (If tomatoes are not full-flavored, you may wish to add more paste.) Add flour and chicken broth, then bring to a boil, stirring constantly. Puree in a blender, then strain to remove seeds and skins. Add 1–2 cups light cream.

Reheat to serve, but do not boil. Add sherry to taste. This soup keeps very well and may be frozen.

Note: If flavorful tomatoes are not at hand, you may substitute a 28-ounce can Italian tomatoes, drained.

20 MUSHROOM and CHIVE BISQUE

Serves
4 to 6
. . . just what you have been looking for to justify that lush pot of chives sitting on the window sill.

Preparation
15 minutes

1½ pounds mushrooms
½ cup butter
¼ cup flour
¼ teaspoon dry mustard
2 cups chicken broth
2 cups light cream
⅓ cup minced chives
¼ cup sherry (optional)
1 teaspoon salt or to taste
¼ cup heavy cream, whipped

Wipe mushrooms clean and finely chop, stems and all. (A food processor would be ideal.) In a large, heavy saucepan, melt butter and sauté mushrooms until soft. Add flour and mustard, cooking and stirring for a minute or so. Add chicken broth and cook until thickened, blending with a whisk. Add light cream and chives, reserving some of the chives for garnish. Flavor with sherry, if desired, and salt to taste.

Serve hot or cold, garnishing each soup bowl with a dollop of whipped cream and a sprinkling of the reserved chives. (You'll be delighted to find that the soup is even better the next day!)

There's a nutty quality that makes this delightfully and deliciously different. Let it begin a spectacular dinner party or serve it as a supper soup.

Serves
8 to 12

Cooking
50 minutes

Preparation
20 minutes

 ⅔ cup raw wild rice
 2 cups water
 ½ teaspoon salt
 2 medium leeks
 2–3 large mushrooms
 ½ cup butter
 ½ cup flour
 2 quarts chicken broth
 1 cup light cream
 3 tablespoons dry sherry
 Salt and pepper to taste
 Minced parsley

Thoroughly wash rice and place in a heavy saucepan with water and salt. Bring to a boil and simmer, covered, until tender but not too soft; about 45 minutes. Fluff with a fork and simmer another 5 minutes, uncovered. Drain well.

Wash and trim leeks, leaving some of the green part. Chop leeks and mushrooms and sauté in butter in a large saucepan until just tender; about 3 minutes. Stirring with a wooden spoon, sprinkle in flour and cook 1 minute. Slowly add chicken broth, blending well, and then rice. Stir with a whisk until thickened, then blend in cream and sherry. Remove from heat before it comes to a boil. Season with salt and pepper to taste.

Sprinkle each serving with minced parsley.

22 PISTOU SOUP

Serves 12

*Preparation
3 hours*

Don't let this recipe terrify you. A version of a celebrated Genoese soup, it is not difficult and is particularly delicious when prepared a day ahead. Fun to do on a dreary Saturday afternoon for Sunday's special supper.

¾ cup dried navy beans, rinsed
3 cups water

Boil beans in water for 2 minutes. Remove from heat and let soak for 1 hour. Return to heat and simmer, covered, for 1–1½ hours or until tender.

1 large onion, chopped
¼ cup olive oil
1 pound fresh tomatoes, peeled and chopped
1 quart beef broth
1 quart chicken broth
1 quart water
1½ cups diced carrots
1½ cups diced red potatoes (unpeeled)
2 leeks, coarsely chopped
½ cup coarsely chopped celery leaves
1½ teaspoons salt
Freshly ground pepper to taste

While beans are soaking, in a large soup kettle sauté onion in olive oil until soft. Add tomatoes and gently cook 3–4 minutes. Add remaining ingredients and heat to boiling. Immediately reduce heat and simmer, uncovered, 15 minutes.

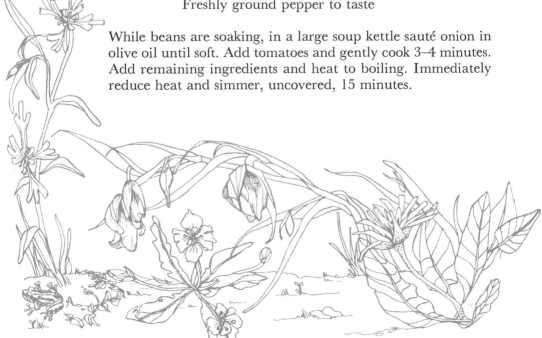

½ pound green beans, sliced ⅛-inch thick
   crosswise
2 medium zucchinis, diced
1 bunch spinach, coarsely chopped
1 cup broken, dried vermicelli or thin noodles
2 pinches crumbled saffron thread
2 hot Italian sausages, chopped
1 6-ounce package sliced corned beef

When navy beans are cooked and tender, add to soup kettle with their liquid. Add green beans, zucchini, spinach, vermicelli, and saffron. Simmer 15 minutes more or until vegetables are tender. In a skillet, sauté chopped sausage until done, then drain on paper toweling. Cut corned beef into thin strips and add to soup with drained sausage.

PISTOU

6 cloves garlic
⅓ cup dried basil
1 6-ounce can tomato paste
½ cup freshly grated Parmesan cheese
¼ cup olive oil

Prepare pistou in a food processor by chopping garlic first then adding basil, tomato paste, and cheese. Slowly blend in oil. You will have a thick, pasty mixture. Thin with 1 cup of the soup stock, then stir all into soup. *Finis*!

As a one-dish meal for a wintry night, serve with hot, crusty PEASANT BREAD from our first *Private Collection* and pass lots of freshly grated Parmesan cheese.

23 PASTA SALAD

Serves 10

Preparation 45 minutes

We would be remiss not to include a pasta salad, so we made sure that this one is the best! The vegetables are stir-fried to ensure bright colors and perfect texture. The dressing is ideally proportioned.

> 1 pound fusilli, shell, or bow-tie pasta
> ½ green bell pepper, cut in thin strips
> ½ red bell pepper, cut in thin strips
> ½ red onion, cut in thin strips
> 1½ tablespoons oil, plus
> ¼ pound mushrooms, sliced
> 1 cup broccoli florets
> 2 small zucchini, cut in half lengthwise and sliced
> 12 fresh asparagus tips*
> 1 basket cherry tomatoes, cut in half
> 1 6-ounce jar marinated artichoke hearts, undrained
> Salt and freshly ground pepper to taste

Prepare pasta to "al dente" stage (still firm to the bite), according to package directions.

In a large skillet, sauté pepper and onion in oil. When peppers just begin to soften, add sliced mushrooms and stir-fry until slightly cooked. Remove to a large bowl. Stir-fry broccoli for 1–2 minutes, adding another tablespoon of oil if necessary. Add zucchini and cook until tender but still crisp. Add to vegetables in bowl. Stir-fry asparagus tips, adding a touch more oil if necessary. As soon as they turn bright green, remove to bowl.

Add cherry tomato halves and undrained artichoke hearts to bowl. Season all with salt and freshly ground pepper to taste.

DRESSING

   ½ cup parsley leaves
   1 cup fresh basil leaves (or 2 tablespoons dried)
   2 cloves garlic
   2 tablespoons olive oil

   ½ cup olive oil
   ½ cup red wine vinegar
   1 tablespoon dried oregano
   1 teaspoon salt
   1 teaspoon freshly ground pepper

Combine parsley, basil, garlic, and 2 tablespoons oil in a food processor or blender until well-chopped. Add to rest of dressing ingredients.

   1–2 teaspoons butter
   ⅓–½ cup pine nuts
   ½ cup freshly grated Parmesan cheese

Sauté pine nuts in butter until brown. Drain on paper toweling. Combine pasta, vegetables, dressing, and Parmesan cheese. Toss gently but well. Correct seasoning and place in a handsome bowl or platter. Top with pine nuts. Fresh basil leaves would be an attractive garnish.

*Note: Chinese pea pods, sugar snap peas, or green beans are nice substitutes for asparagus. Also, if you should be fortunate enough to have any left-over salad, additional Parmesan cheese would freshen it.

24 PATIO SALAD

Serves 8

*Preparation
30 minutes*

*Marinate
3–24 hours*

Here is a California menu in every sense, and thus ideal for warm, summer days or evenings. The salad is a complete meal in itself, but CALIFORNIA ORANGE SOUP and CHAPATIS (Indian bread) would dress it up for special luncheons or outdoor suppers.

2 cups chicken broth
1 teaspoon instant chicken bouillon
1 cup bulghur wheat

Bring broth and bouillon to a boil and stir in bulghur wheat. Reduce heat, cover, and simmer 15 minutes. Partially cool.

DRESSING

1 cup mayonnaise
1 cup yogurt
¼ cup salad oil
¼ cup lemon juice
4 teaspoons Dijon mustard
1 clove garlic, minced
1 teaspoon oregano
1 teaspoon basil
½ teaspoon freshly ground pepper

Combine the above ingredients to make a dressing. Add 1 cup of it to the partially cooled bulghur wheat; cover and refrigerate for several hours or overnight. Refrigerate the remaining dressing until serving time.

1 cup shredded carrots
1 cup thinly sliced celery
1 bunch green onions, chopped
½ cup chopped parsley
Garnishes (see below)

Combine above ingredients (except garnishes) with the marinated bulghur wheat. Turn onto a large serving platter, then use your imagination in surrounding it with all sorts of beautiful garnishes: *quartered hard-cooked eggs, tomato wedges, chunks of Monterey jack* or *Swiss cheese, julienne chicken* and *ham, blanched florets of broccoli* and *cauliflower, blanched sugar peas,* and *sliced, raw mushrooms.* Pass the reserved dressing for those who might wish an extra sauce for the vegetables.

CRAB MEAT MOUSSE 25

Delicate and pretty for a summer luncheon.

Serves 6

2 cups Alaska King crab meat, flaked
2 tablespoons lime or lemon juice
2 tablespoons unflavored gelatin
1 cup cold water
1 cup boiling water
1 cup mayonnaise
1 cup heavy cream, whipped
Pimento strips and watercress

Preparation
15 minutes

Chill

Toss crab meat in lime juice and set aside. In a medium-sized bowl, soak gelatin in cold water for 5 minutes. Add boiling water and let cool. Whisk in mayonnaise and whipped cream, then crab meat. Pour into a 6-cup mold or 6 individual molds. Chill. Decorate with pimento strips and watercress.

SOUR CREAM DRESSING

1 cup sour cream
2 tablespoons vinegar
1 large cucumber, finely diced
1 clove garlic, minced
Salt, pepper, and paprika to taste

Combine dressing ingredients, seasoning to taste. Pour into a sauce bowl to accompany the mousse.

Serve with COLD GREEN BEANS AND CARROTS and WATERCRESS SANDWICHES, then LEMON DAINTY with raspberries for dessert.

26 FETTUCINE in BASIL CREAM

Serves
4 to 6

Preparation
15 minutes

This is a very attractive pasta dish. For a colorful addition, consider a cup or two of fresh asparagus tips and/or a quarter-pound of lobster or crab meat.

3 tablespoons olive oil
3 tablespoons butter
1–2 cloves garlic, minced
3–4 tomatoes, peeled, seeded, and chopped
½ cup dry white wine
½ cup heavy cream
½ cup finely chopped fresh basil leaves
Salt and white pepper to taste
1 pound fettucine (fresh is best!)
Freshly grated Parmesan cheese

Heat oil and butter in a heavy saucepan over medium heat. Gently sauté garlic for a minute, then add tomatoes. Simmer until they soften, then add wine and cream. Simmer 5–10 minutes or until sauce becomes consistency of heavy cream. Add chopped basil and simmer another 2–3 minutes. Add salt and white pepper to taste.

In a large kettle, cook the fettucine in boiling, salted water with a tablespoon of oil. When it has reached the "al dente" stage (still firm to the bite), drain immediately.

Add the sauce to the hot fettucine, toss, and serve immediately on warm plates. Add a leaf or two of basil to each serving for a pretty touch. Pass a bowl of freshly grated Parmesan cheese.

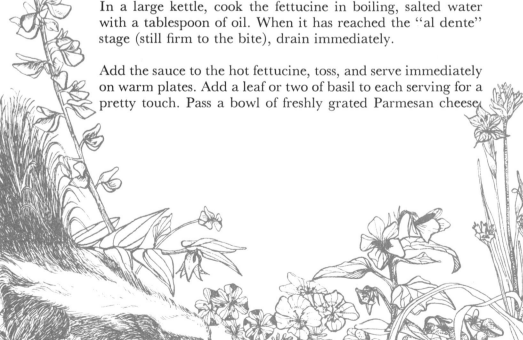

It's beautiful!

Serves 6

1½ pounds asparagus
1½ pounds medium to large raw shrimp
¼ cup peanut oil
1 onion, sliced
4 teaspoons soy sauce
1 tablespoon toasted sesame seeds
1 teaspoon salt (optional)

*Preparation
30 minutes*

Wash and trim asparagus. Cut into 2-inch pieces, discarding tough ends. Shell and devein shrimp.

Heat oil in a large skillet or wok over medium-high heat. Stir-fry asparagus, shrimp, and onion until shrimp are pink and vegetables tender-crisp; about 3–5 minutes. Stir in soy sauce, sesame seeds, and salt. Serve with steamed rice.

28 NAPA CABBAGE and CRAB

Serves
4 to 6

Preparation
15 minutes

Another intriguing recipe to emerge from one of Mr. Zeu Lien Loo's unforgettable cooking classes of years gone by. The mild, delicate sweetness of napa cabbage (also known as Chinese or celery cabbage) is just right with crab. In oriental fashion, assemble all of your ingredients ahead of time so that you have only a few minutes away from your guests before serving.

1 2-pound head of napa cabbage
2 green onions, chopped
1 tablespoon minced fresh ginger root
1 clove garlic, minced
1 teaspoon brown sugar
½ teaspoon salt
½ teaspoon white pepper
1 pound crab meat
1½ teaspoons cornstarch
2 teaspoons water
½ cup chicken broth
¼ cup sherry
3 tablespoons peanut oil
Pinch of salt
Pinch of sugar

Remove stem of cabbage and quarter head lengthwise. Cut large leaves in fourths but leave small, center leaves whole.

Combine onions, ginger, garlic, brown sugar, salt, and white pepper. Toss with crab meat. Combine cornstarch and water. Have chicken broth and sherry at hand.

Ten minutes before serving time, preheat wok or large skillet over high heat. Add oil, along with pinches of salt and sugar, and heat until rippling. Swish oil around wok and add cabbage. Stir-fry for 2–3 minutes, then add chicken broth and sherry. Reduce heat to medium and stir for 1 minute. Add cornstarch mixture and stir until thickened.

Serve over steaming hot rice. For a bright green accent, accompany it with crisp-tender broccoli and Chinese pea pods, tossed together with a little melted butter and a sprinkling of lemon juice.

One of our contributing cooks claims that this recipe is so good, *Serves 2*
she dreams about it! You'll find that's probably true.

Preparation
20 minutes

> 2 fresh trout, boned and butterflied
>   (about 10–12 ounces each)
> Flour
> 4 tablespoons butter
> 3 tablespoons sliced almonds
> ½ cup almond liqueur
> Juice of 1 lemon
> Salt and freshly ground pepper to taste
> ⅔ cup heavy cream

Preheat broiler, placing rack about 8 inches below.

Dredge trout in flour, shaking off excess. Heat butter to
bubbling stage in a 12-inch skillet (this is the time to use that
good-looking copper skillet!). Place trout in pan, skin-side up.
Sauté over medium-high heat for 2–3 minutes or until golden
brown. Remove from heat.

Carefully turn trout over with 2 spatulas. Sprinkle with almonds and place under broiler. Broil until almonds are
browned, then return skillet to top of stove. Sauté for another
minute or two, then remove from heat. Add almond liqueur
and flame, shaking pan until flame dies. Return to heat and
add lemon juice, salt and pepper. Add cream. Shake pan well
until sauce has thickened. Serve at once.

To complete your dinner, we suggest APRICOT AND PINE NUT
PILAF and a pretty green salad or SICILIAN BROCCOLI.

30 RED SNAPPER with PINEAPPLE

Serves
4 to 6

Preparation
30 minutes

Beautiful colors and flavors.

1½ pounds red snapper fillets
1 teaspoon turmeric
1½ teaspoons salt
3 tablespoons peanut oil
2 onions, finely chopped
1½ inches ginger root, peeled and finely chopped
2 jalapeño chilies, seeded and finely chopped
1 teaspoon grated lemon rind
1 teaspoon turmeric
1 teaspoon sugar
4 tomatoes, peeled, seeded, and coarsely chopped
Half of a fresh pineapple, cut in chunks

Wash and pat dry fish. Combine turmeric and salt on a sheet of waxed paper, and pat into fish. Cut each fillet crosswise into 2-inch wide strips.

Heat wok or a large, heavy skillet over medium-high to high heat. Add oil. When it begins to ripple, add fish. Fry for 4–5 minutes, removing as soon as fish is cooked through.

Reduce heat to medium, adding more oil if necessary. Sauté onions until soft. Add ginger, chilies, lemon, and turmeric. Cook 2 minutes then stir in rest of ingredients. Simmer 2–3 minutes, then return fish to pan to heat through.

Serve with rice. MARY LIZ'S SPINACH SALAD would be lovely with this.

HALIBUT with ROSEMARY 31

Understatement is what makes this so special.

Serves 4

1 ½ pounds halibut steaks
Juice of 2–3 limes
Salt and freshly ground pepper
Flour
2 tablespoons olive oil
¼ cup white wine vinegar
2 tablespoons water
3 cloves garlic, lightly pounded
½ teaspoon crushed rosemary

*Marinate
1–2 hours*

*Preparation
20 minutes*

In a shallow, glass dish, marinate halibut in lime juice for 1–2 hours. Wipe with a paper towel. Sprinkle with salt and pepper, and dredge with flour, shaking off excess.

Heat oil in a 12-inch skillet until it ripples. Add fish and brown on both sides; about 5 minutes per side or until it flakes. Transfer to warm serving platter and cover with foil.

Add vinegar and water to pan drippings. When sizzling stops, add garlic and rosemary. Simmer briskly until reduced to half, stirring and scraping to blend. Discard garlic cloves. Spoon mixture over fish.

Serve with GRITS SOUFFLÉ and SWISS CHARD.

32 SCALLOPS of SALMON in LIME CREAM

Serves 6

*Preparation
30 minutes*

*Marinate
1 hour*

So elegant and surprisingly easy. Use your prettiest silver platter, lavishly embellished with watercress and paper-thin slices of lime.

Half of a 10-pound salmon, boned
Salt and white pepper
Juice of 2 limes
2 limes
4 tablespoons butter
⅓ cup dry vermouth
1 cup heavy cream
Watercress and lime slices

Try to talk your fishmonger into preparing the salmon scallops for you. Otherwise, use pliers to pull any remaining bones from fish. Starting near tail end, at a 30-degree angle, cut fillet into 1-inch thick slices. You should have about 12 in all. Lightly season with salt and white pepper. Place in a shallow, glass dish along with the juice of 2 limes. Marinate at room temperature for 1 hour, turning several times.

Meanwhile, use a vegetable peeler to remove the outer skin of 2 limes. Cut the peel into thin strips (julienne) and place in a small saucepan with cold water to cover. Bring to a boil, then immediately drain and rinse in cold water to retain the marvelous green color. Dry on paper toweling and set aside in plastic wrap. Section the limes, removing membrane. Reserve.

Ten minutes before serving time, drain salmon on paper towels. In a 12-inch skillet, gently sauté the julienne lime in butter for ½ minute. Increase heat to medium-high and add some of the salmon scallops. (Do not crowd pan. This should be done in 2–3 batches.) Sauté 1–2 minutes on each side, depending on thickness of fish. Remove to a warm platter and cover.

Leaving julienne lime in pan, pour off all but 1 tablespoon of butter. Add vermouth and cream, blending with a flat whisk, then add reserved lime sections. Simmer for 2–3 minutes over medium heat to slightly thicken. Season to taste with salt and white pepper.

Pour sauce over scallops and garnish platter with watercress and lime slices. We found a delicious menu to be buttered brown and wild rice tossed together, and TOMATOES FILLED WITH BROCCOLI.

33 LEMON CHICKEN BROCHETTES

Serves 4

*Preparation
30 minutes*

*Marinate
1–2 hours*

*Barbecue
30 minutes*

These are pretty, easy, appealing to all ages . . . ideal for the first spring barbecue.

    1½ pounds boned and skinned chicken breasts
    3 small zucchini, unpeeled
    ½ pound whole mushrooms

Cut breasts (about 5 halves) into 2-inch wide pieces; about 3–4 per breast. Slice zucchini 1-inch thick. Alternate chicken, zucchini, and mushrooms on skewers, keeping everything about the same thickness for even cooking. Place in a shallow, glass dish for marinating.

    Juice of 3 lemons
    1 tablespoon grated lemon peel
    ¼ cup olive oil
    1 tablespoon sugar
    1 tablespoon cider vinegar
    1 clove garlic, minced
    2 teaspoons salt
    ¼ teaspoon cayenne pepper

Combine above ingredients and pour over brochettes. Cover and let sit at room temperature for 1–2 hours, turning periodically. (Refrigerate if any longer.)

Slowly barbecue brochettes over medium coals for 25–30 minutes, turning periodically. Baste with marinade. Serve on beds of rice, holding meat down with a fork while withdrawing skewers. Provide individual bowls of the following butter sauce for dipping.

    ¼ cup melted butter
    1 tablespoon lemon juice
    1 tablespoon chopped parsley
    Dash of cayenne pepper

HERBED CHERRY TOMATOES and fresh asparagus are just right with this. Pass a basket of hot SOUR CREAM BISCUITS.

Think of this for an intimate supper for four . . . the kind one pictures in a rustic setting before a crackling fire with a wonderful jug of wine.

Serves 4

Preparation 15 minutes

Baking 1½ hours

    1 plump broiling chicken, quartered
    3 tablespoons oil
    ½ teaspoon thyme
    ½ teaspoon oregano
    ½ teaspoon savory
    1 bouquet garni of parsley, celery, bay leaf, and leek
    4 heads garlic, unpeeled

Preheat oven to 350°.

Wash and thoroughly dry chicken. Place in a heavy, earthenware casserole that has a lid. Add oil, thyme, oregano, and savory, then turn chicken pieces to coat well.

Tie together a large bouquet of parsley sprigs, a small celery stalk or two, a bay leaf, and a small leek, root and all. Place in center of casserole and surround with chicken. Break apart garlic heads and place unpeeled cloves in all interstices of chicken.

Make a luting paste of ⅓ cup flour, 2–3 tablespoons water, and a teaspoon or so of oil. Place lid on top of casserole and seal with paste. Bake 1½ hours.

The fun is in not breaking the seal until the casserole is on the table. You'll delight in the sudden rush of delicious smells. Just push the bouquet and garlic cloves aside, when serving.

Serve a hearty dish with this such as ITALIAN POTATOES. We also like HOT AND COLD SALAD.

35 BEBE'S CHICKEN CURRY

Serves 6

*Preparation
45 minutes*

"Bebe was a friend of ours from southern India who lived in our apartment building during our stay in England. This is her fabulous dish." Serve the CURRY over rice with CHAPATIS (Indian Bread), and COCONUT MOLD for dessert to create a spectacular menu. We suggest that you prepare the entire menu in the morning or the day before. You'll be pleased by how easy it all is.

2 large onions, chopped
3 tablespoons oil
4 cloves garlic, minced
2 teaspoons freshly grated ginger root
1–2 teaspoons curry powder
1–1½ teaspoons chili powder
¼ teaspoon ground cloves
¼ teaspoon cardamom
¼ teaspoon turmeric
2–2½ pounds chicken breasts, cubed
2 tablespoons curry paste*
½ cup water
2 tomatoes, peeled and sliced
¾ cup coconut milk*
⅓ cup golden raisins
1½ tablespoons lemon juice
Salt to taste
Bananas, cilantro sprigs, and chutney (optional)

Reserve ½ cup of chopped onions for the YOGURT SAUCE. In a 12-inch, heavy skillet, heat oil and sauté the remaining onion, garlic, ginger, curry powder, chili powder, ground cloves, cardamom, and turmeric. When onions are soft, add cubed chicken and sauté until lightly browned. Add curry paste, water, and tomatoes. Simmer until chicken is done, stirring periodically; about 7–10 minutes. Remove from heat and add coconut milk, raisins, lemon juice, and salt to taste.

To serve, reheat curry but do not boil. Spoon over steaming hot rice on individual plates, garnishing each with a lengthwise slice of banana and sprigs of cilantro (Chinese parsley). Pass chutney, warm CHAPATIS, and the following sauce.

YOGURT SAUCE

2 cups yogurt
¾ cup shredded coconut
1 tomato, diced
½ cucumber, diced
½ cup reserved chopped onion
2 jalapeño chilies, chopped
2 teaspoons freshly grated ginger root

Combine above ingredients and let stand several hours.

*Note: Curry powder may be substituted for the paste, but the latter is preferred. You can purchase canned or frozen coconut milk, or you may puree ¼ cup dried, shredded coconut with 1 cup hot milk in a blender and strain.

CHAPATIS 36

After the required 6 hours of standing, these may be rolled out, stacked, and refrigerated until time to fry.

Yield 12
Serves 6

2 cups self-rising flour
2½ tablespoons yogurt
1½ teaspoons cumin seeds
½ teaspoon salt
½ cup water

Preparation
10 minutes

Rising
6 hours

In a bowl, combine all ingredients at once with a wooden spoon. Knead in bowl for a minute or two, until dough becomes elastic. Cover bowl with plastic film and let sit at room temperature for 6 hours. (Do not expect much rising.)

Cooking
2 minutes

Divide dough into 12 balls. On lightly floured board, roll out into 6-inch circles. At this point, chapatis may be refrigerated.

Just before serving time, pour cooking oil into a large, heavy skillet to ¼-inch depth. When oil is hot, fry chapatis on each side until browned and puffed. Drain on paper toweling. Serve immediately in a napkin-lined basket.

37 CHICKEN BREASTS in PHYLLO

Serves 12

*Preparation
30 minutes*

*Baking
20–25
minutes*

These are a caterer's delight! Surprisingly easy to prepare in quantity, they may be kept frozen until the day of the party. The phyllo-wrapped breasts are elegant looking. For a dinner party, we suggest MUSHROOM SOUFFLÉ, GINGERED CARROTS, and WATERCRESS AND ENDIVE SALAD. A lovely luncheon could include MOLDED SPINACH ON TOMATO RINGS (from our first *Private Collection*) and MANDARIN SALAD.

1½ cups mayonnaise
1 cup chopped green onion
⅓ cup lemon juice
2 cloves garlic, minced
2 teaspoons dry tarragon

12 chicken breast halves, boned and skinned
Salt and pepper
24 sheets phyllo dough (see index)
1⅓ cups butter, melted
⅓ cup freshly grated Parmesan cheese

Combine first 5 ingredients to make a sauce. Lightly sprinkle chicken pieces with salt and pepper. Place a sheet of phyllo on working surface. Quickly brush with melted butter (about 2 teaspoons). Place a second sheet on top of first. Brush with melted butter. Spread about 1½ tablespoons of sauce on each side of a chicken breast (3 tablespoons in all). Place breast in one corner of buttered phyllo sheets. Fold corner over breast, then fold sides over and roll breast up in the sheets to form a package. Place in an ungreased baking dish. Repeat with remaining breasts and phyllo sheets.

Brush packets with rest of butter and sprinkle with Parmesan cheese. At this point, the dish may be tightly sealed and frozen. Thaw completely before baking.

Bake at 375° for 20–25 minutes, or until golden. Serve hot.

This is superb . . . a delicate dish with unusual flavors, and a breeze to prepare for special guests.

Serves
4 to 6

Preparation
15 minutes

Baking
10–15
minutes

> 3 whole chicken breasts, boned, skinned, and split*
> 1 teaspoon cinnamon
> ½ teaspoon garlic salt
> ¼ teaspoon allspice
> ¼ teaspoon nutmeg
> ¼ teaspoon white pepper
> 1 tablespoon butter
> 1 tablespoon oil
> 2 tablespoons chopped chives
> ⅔ cup heavy cream
> ½ cup dry vermouth
> Chopped parsley or watercress sprigs

*To ensure the delicate quality of the suprêmes, it is *very* important that the breasts be at room temperature before preparing.

Preheat oven to 300°. Wash and dry chicken. Mix the 5 seasonings together on a sheet of waxed paper then pat into breasts. Heat butter and oil in a heavy skillet. Sauté breasts over medium-low to low heat for 1 minute per side, just until opaque. Place in a shallow baking dish and bake, uncovered, for 10 minutes (15 minutes, if breasts are very thick).

Using same skillet, sauté chives for a half minute. Add cream and vermouth, stirring with a flat whisk. Increase heat to medium and let simmer several minutes to thicken slightly.

Place chicken on a warm platter, pour sauce over, and sprinkle with chopped parsley or sprigs of watercress.

As a menu suggestion, try simply prepared brown or wild rice, and baby carrots tossed with 2 tablespoons butter, 2 tablespoons orange marmalade, and a dash of nutmeg or powdered ginger.

39 CHICKEN PONTALBA

At first glance, this may seem overwhelming, but we assure you that the preparation is quite simple and the results are spectacular. The ham mixture and Bearnaise sauce may be done a day ahead or in the morning. The potatoes can be diced and set aside in a bowl of salted water for several hours before baking. The chicken may be browned up to 2 hours in advance.

HAM MIXTURE

¼ cup butter
2 medium onions, chopped
1 cup (¼ pound) finely chopped mushrooms
¾ cup finely chopped green onions
2–3 cloves garlic, minced
½ pound ham, cut in ¼-inch cubes
1 cup dry white wine
¼ cup finely chopped parsley

Melt butter in a heavy, 10-inch skillet. Over medium heat, sauté onions, mushrooms, green onions, and garlic until onions are soft; about 3–5 minutes. Any liquid in pan should have evaporated before adding ham. Lightly brown ham, stirring, then add wine and parsley. Increase heat and stir constantly until liquid is absorbed. Remove from heat immediately.

BEARNAISE SAUCE

1 cup butter, melted
4 egg yolks
2 tablespoons lemon juice
Pinch of salt and cayenne pepper

1 tablespoon tarragon vinegar
2 tablespoons white wine
1 teaspoon dried tarragon, crumbled
2 teaspoons chopped shallots
Freshly ground pepper

Heat butter. Place egg yolks, lemon juice, salt, and cayenne pepper in electric blender. Cover and turn to high. Immediately remove cover and add *hot* butter in a steady stream.

In a small skillet, bring remaining ingredients to a boil and reduce to 1 tablespoon. Add to blender and whirl. (If made ahead and chilled, just set over hot water to warm.)

> 4 cups diced, unpeeled, red-skinned potatoes
> (¼-inch dice)
> 3 tablespoons butter, melted
> Salt and pepper
> Paprika

Dice potatoes and set aside in a bowl of salted water until 30 minutes before serving.

Preheat oven to 450°. Pat potatoes dry in a towel, then toss in melted butter in a shallow pan. Spread out in a single layer. Lightly salt and pepper, then give a generous sprinkling of paprika. Bake until nicely browned and crisp; about 20–30 minutes.

> 3 pounds chicken breasts (4 large), boned,
> skinned, and halved
> Flour
> Salt and freshly ground pepper
> ¼–½ cup butter

Lightly dredge breasts in flour seasoned with salt and pepper. When potatoes are placed in oven, melt butter in a 12-inch skillet over medium heat. Lightly but evenly brown breasts. Reduce heat to low, cover, and cook until *just* done; about 5–10 minutes, depending on thickness of breasts.

When ready to serve, combine ham mixture (gently reheated, if necessary) with potatoes and spoon onto serving platter or divide between heated dinner plates. Top with chicken breasts. Pour Bearnaise sauce over breasts and serve immediately. TOMATOES FILLED WITH BROCCOLI and PARTY ROLLS (from our first *Private Collection*), then ORANGES IN GRAND MARNIER for dessert, create a splendid menu.

40 ROCK CORNISH GAME HENS in GRAPE SAUCE

Serves 6

Preparation
20 minutes

Marinate
2–3 hours

Baking
1 hour

The hens stay moist and tender, and the fresh flavors and aromas are delightful. For a simpler meal, you may wish to omit the sauce.

> 3 game hens
> ¼ cup olive oil
> Juice of 2–3 limes
> 2 tablespoons minced fresh sage leaves
> 2 tablespoons chopped mint leaves
> 2 cloves garlic, minced
> 1 teaspoon salt
> ½ teaspoon freshly ground pepper
> 3 drops Tabasco sauce

Split hens in half. Wash and dry well. Place in a shallow, 9 x 13-inch, glass baking dish. Combine remaining ingredients and pour over hens. Cover and refrigerate 2–3 hours, turning hens in marinade several times.

Preheat oven to 450°. Uncover hens and roast in marinade for 20 minutes. Reduce temperature to 400°. Bake 30–40 minutes more, or until hens are golden brown and tender, basting every 10–15 minutes. Transfer to serving platter, cover, and keep warm.

GRAPE SAUCE

> 1 cup chicken broth, heated
> ½ cup tawny port wine
> 2 tablespoons cornstarch, dissolved in
> 2 tablespoons water
> 1 tablespoon brown sugar
> 1 teaspoon fresh thyme leaves (¼ teaspoon dried)
> 2 cups seedless red grapes

Add hot chicken broth to juices in baking dish and stir to loosen brown particles. Pour into a saucepan and add wine, cornstarch/water mixture, sugar, thyme, and grapes. Cook, stirring, over high heat until mixture thickens and clears.

Pour half of sauce over hens and the rest into a sauceboat. Garnish the platter with clusters of fresh grapes and sprigs of mint. Serve with BROWN BUTTER RICE and ENDIVE AND WATER-CRESS SALAD.

Note: For a spring menu, you might like to substitute green seedless grapes and white wine.

41 RABBIT in CREAM SAUCE with SHALLOTS

Serves 4

*Preparation
30 minutes*

*Cooking
1–1½ hours*

If you have one of those beautiful, oval, copper skillets, use it to prepare and serve this superb dish, dressing it with bouquets of fresh thyme.

1 2½–3 pound fresh rabbit, cut in pieces
Salt and pepper
3 tablespoons butter
1 tablespoon oil
½ cup cognac
1 tablespoon butter
⅔ pound shallots, finely chopped
1 cup dry white wine
1 bay leaf
5 sprigs of fresh thyme (or ½ teaspoon dried)
⅓–½ cup crème fraîche*
Salt and freshly ground pepper to taste

Season rabbit pieces with salt and pepper. Over medium-high heat, melt 3 tablespoons butter with oil in a 12-inch skillet until sizzling. Add rabbit pieces and brown until golden. Remove pieces and turn off heat (if using gas) before adding cognac. Immediately flame cognac. As flame dies, stir to loosen brown particles. Turn heat back on to medium, add another tablespoon of butter and the shallots. Simmer for about 3 minutes or until shallots are soft and golden.

Return rabbit to pan and add wine, bay leaf, and thyme. Cover and let simmer slowly for 1–1½ hours, until rabbit is tender.

When done, remove rabbit to a warm platter, discarding bay leaf and thyme sprigs. With a flat whisk, stir crème fraîche into pan juices. Simmer a few minutes then check seasoning for salt and pepper.

Serve in that handsome skillet or place rabbit on a warm, silver platter, pouring cream sauce over. Excellent with rice, baby carrots, and MINTED PEAS.**

*To make crème fraîche, add 1 teaspoon buttermilk per 1 cup heavy (whipping) cream. Let stand, covered, at room temperature for 8–12 hours, until thickened. Stir, cover, and refrigerate. It will keep at least 2 weeks. (If you do not have crème fraîche available at last minute, you may substitute 1 tablespoon sour cream combined with ½ cup heavy cream.)

**MINTED PEAS: Add 1 tablespoon chopped mint leaves and 1 teaspoon lime juice to 2–3 tablespoons melted butter, with a good pinch of sugar. Just before serving, toss with peas, adding salt and pepper to taste.

42 VEAL TENDERLOINS with TOMATOES and CREAM

Serves 6

*Preparation
15 minutes*

*Baking
45 minutes*

If you are looking for an unusual meat course, we think this will appeal. You probably should contact your butcher ahead of time to order the tenderloins, since they are considered a delicacy. This is another one of those delicious dishes that may be prepared well in advance.

2 whole veal tenderloins (about 1 pound each)
Flour seasoned with salt and pepper
2 tablespoons butter
1 pound mushrooms, sliced
1 tablespoon butter
2 cups heavy cream
2 teaspoons Dijon mustard
1½ teaspoons salt
4 tomatoes, peeled
1–2 tablespoons freshly grated Parmesan cheese

Preheat oven to 400°.

Dredge tenderloins in seasoned flour, shaking off excess. In a large, heavy skillet, brown meat in 2 tablespoons butter over medium-high heat. Transfer to a shallow casserole.

Sauté mushrooms in pan drippings, adding another tablespoon of butter. When just tender, pour over meat. Combine cream, mustard, and salt, and pour over mushrooms. Cut peeled tomatoes into wedges, and arrange around veal. Top with Parmesan cheese. At this point, the dish may be set aside or refrigerated until an hour before baking time. Bake, uncovered, for 45 minutes.

You may either carve the meat at the table or do so in the kitchen, reassembling the tenderloins and serving in their casserole or on a warm platter, surrounded with the vegetables and sauce. Serve with a rice dish and a simple green vegetable, such as RISOTTO ALLA MILANESE and FRESH GREEN BEANS from our first *Private Collection*.

This menu is a harried hostess's dream. All may be prepared many hours ahead to create an exquisite dinner.

Serves
6 to 8

2 pounds veal scallops
Flour
½ cup butter
½ cup dry white wine
¼ cup lemon juice
1 clove garlic, minced
Salt and pepper to taste
½ pound mushrooms, sliced
1 bunch green onions, thinly sliced
Chopped parsley

Preparation
20 minutes

Baking
30 minutes

Dredge veal scallops in flour, shaking off excess. Melt butter in a heavy, 12-inch skillet, over medium-high heat. When bubbling, brown veal in 2 batches, sautéeing 1 minute per side.

Returning all meat to pan, add wine, lemon juice, garlic, and salt and pepper. Reduce heat to medium and let simmer for a minute.

At this point, all may be transferred to a casserole (or left in skillet) and refrigerated until an hour or so before serving time. Let veal return to room temperature before baking. Top with sliced mushrooms and green onions. Bake, covered, at 350° for 30 minutes. Sprinkle with chopped parsley before serving.

For wonderful ease, serve with GRITS SOUFFLÉ, GINGERED CAR-ROTS, and ENDIVE AND WATERCRESS SALAD.

44 RAGOUT of PORK in WHITE WINE

Ragout is a derivative of the French verb, ragoûter . . . "to restore the appetite of." This recipe will do just that! Make a day or two ahead for even better flavor.

3 tablespoons oil
2 pounds boneless pork shoulder, cut in 1-inch cubes
1 large onion, chopped
2 cloves garlic, minced
3 tablespoons flour
1¼–1½ cups rich chicken broth
1 cup dry white wine
1 bay leaf
½ teaspoon crumbled rosemary leaves
¼ teaspoon crushed thyme leaves
½ teaspoon salt
¼ teaspoon freshly ground pepper
2 cups sliced carrots (¼-inch thick)

In a large skillet or Dutch oven, heat oil. Brown pork quickly in small batches, setting aside. Add onion and garlic to pan drippings. Sauté until soft and golden. Sprinkle with flour and stir for 1 minute. Stir in chicken broth and wine, plus herbs and seasonings. Cook and stir with a whisk until thickened.

Add pork and simmer, covered, for 1 hour. Stir in carrots and simmer 30 more minutes, covered, adding a little water if necessary.

2 tablespoons butter
1 pound mushrooms, sliced
¼ cup dry white wine
1 tablespoon lemon juice
¼ cup chopped parsley

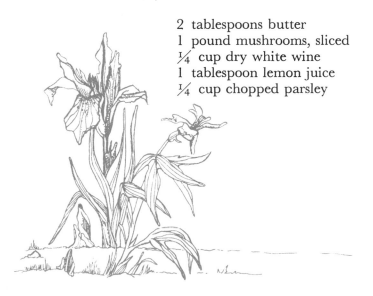

In a large skillet, melt butter and gently sauté mushrooms until soft. Stir into ragout along with wine. Cover and simmer 3 minutes. Stir in lemon juice and sprinkle with chopped parsley.

If you wish, serve with homemade noodles tossed in melted butter with a goodly amount of poppy seeds, and ENDIVE AND WATERCRESS SALAD.

Note: An interesting serving suggestion is to reheat ragout in a large, shallow casserole in a 350° oven. Twenty minutes before serving time, top with HERB BISCUITS (see SOUR CREAM BISCUITS), drizzled with melted butter. Bake until lightly browned.

45 PORK ROAST with CURRANT SAUCE

Serves
8 to 10

Preparation
15 minutes

Marinate
2–3 hours

Roasting
2½–3 hours

Your kitchen will be filled with heavenly aromas!

1 3–4-pound, boned, pork loin roast
½ cup dry sherry
½ cup soy sauce
2 cloves garlic, minced
1 tablespoon dry mustard
1 teaspoon ground ginger
1 teaspoon dried thyme, crushed

Place pork in a plastic bag along with remaining ingredients. Securely tie or seal bag and let sit at room temperature for 2–3 hours, turning occasionally.

Preheat oven to 325°. Reserving marinade, place meat in a shallow baking pan and roast, uncovered, for 2½–3 hours, or until meat thermometer registers 160°–165°. Baste with reserved marinade during last hour. Let roast sit at least 15 minutes before carving.

While the pork is roasting, make the following sauce.

1 10-ounce jar currant jelly
2 tablespoons sherry
1 tablespoon soy sauce
¼ cup dried currants (optional)

Combine above ingredients in a small saucepan over medium-low heat and simmer 2 minutes. If you wish a thicker consistency, serve at room temperature. Otherwise, reheat just before serving. Place in a sauceboat for your guests to pour over meat.

For an absolutely wonderful menu, serve with MUSTARD ASPIC, OVEN-FRIED POTATOES, and SICILIAN BROCCOLI, then ORANGES IN GRAND MARNIER SAUCE for dessert.

Pronounced "fay-zhwah-dah," this version of Rio de Janeiro's celebrated dish was adapted by one of our most creative hostesses to highlight casual parties. She serves it from a handsome tureen, ladling into large, shallow soup bowls filled with fluffy, steamed rice, then garnishing each with juicy orange slices. She insists that only black beans should be used, which can be readily found in specialty markets.

Serves 12 to 14

Soaking overnight

Preparation 15 minutes

Cooking 3–3½ hours

1½–2 pounds black beans
3½ pounds smoked ham hocks
   (quartered by your butcher)
2 pigs' feet (optional)
5–6 garlic (Italian) sausages, cut in 1-inch pieces
3 large garlic cloves
4 bay leaves
Rice
5–6 navel oranges, peeled and sliced ½-inch thick

Rinse beans and cover with several inches of cold water. Soak overnight. Rinse again, removing any dried shells or particles.

In a very large soup kettle or 2 Dutch ovens, combine all ingredients except rice and oranges. Cover with 2 inches or so of water. Bring to a boil and skim off any foam. Reduce heat and simmer, uncovered, for 3–3½ hours. Do not stir. You may have to add more water to keep mixture very "soupy." It must not boil away. Serve as suggested above.

Brazilian in origin, COCONUT MOLD WITH BRANDIED PRUNES would be a superb dessert; or SOUR CREAM ICE CREAM, if time is of the essence.

Note: FEIJOADA, like so many good things, is even better the next day. Gently reheat on top of stove or in a 350° oven. You can not overcook it and it will keep at least 5 days. The leftover beans are delicious pureed in a blender, then heated and served as a thick soup with a garnish of cilantro sprigs.

47 BIGOSZ STEW

Serves 6

Pronounced "bee-gosh," this colorful, sausage stew is an old, Polish family recipe. It's wonderfully easy to prepare before a football game or a long day on the ski slopes. Be sure to buy top-quality sausage.

*Preparation
15 minutes*

*Cooking
2 hours*

4 tablespoons butter
1 large onion, thickly sliced
1 head cabbage, cut in eighths lengthwise
2 pounds Polish sausage, cut in ¼-inch thick slices
2–3 tart green apples, unpeeled
3 tomatoes, unpeeled
2 bay leaves
1 tablespoon white vinegar
Pinch of sugar (optional)

Melt butter in a large, heavy pot or Dutch oven. Sauté onion until soft. Add cabbage slices and sausage. Quarter and core apples, but do not peel. Quarter tomatoes and add to pot with apples, bay leaves, and vinegar. Cover tightly and simmer over low heat for 2 hours.

Before serving, skim any fat from stew, remove bay leaves, and check seasoning. If apples were mildly flavored, you may wish to add a pinch of sugar.

You won't even need a salad with this. Just serve in large bowls with chunks of crusty bread. . . . PEASANT BREAD from our first *Private Collection* would be perfect, along with a crisp chardonnay.

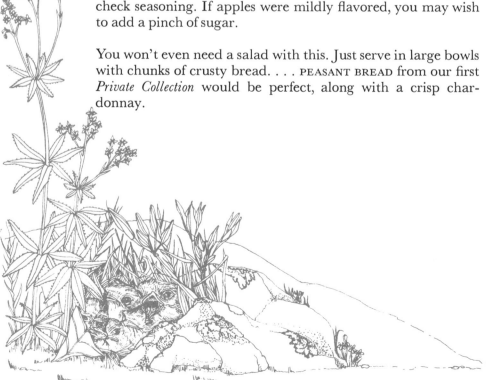

They will turn a casual, spur-of-the-moment supper into a special occasion.

Serves 6

Preparation 15 minutes

Barbecue

4 pita breads
2 pounds ground lamb
1½ cups finely chopped onion
1 cup finely chopped parsley
2 teaspoons salt
1 teaspoon cinnamon
1 teaspoon paprika
½ teaspoon cayenne pepper

Cut each pita bread in half, crosswise, to form a pocket. Wrap pitas in foil and warm in a 300° oven while preparing burgers.

Thoroughly combine remaining ingredients by gently kneading with your fingers. Shape into 8 ½-inch thick, oval patties to accommodate pita halves. Barbecue or broil. (We recommend that burgers be pink in the middle.)

2 cups yogurt
½ cup finely chopped cucumber
1 tablespoon lemon juice
Sliced dill pickles, tomatoes, and red onion

Combine yogurt, cucumber, and lemon juice to serve as a sauce. Let your diners fill each pita half with a burger and choices of sliced pickles, tomatoes, and red onion, then a dollop of sauce.

If you wish, serve with corn-on-the-cob and a tossed green salad, such as the refreshing one in our first *Private Collection*.

49 LEG of LAMB in BURGUNDY

Serves
6 to 8

Preparation
15 minutes

Roasting
2 hours

This almost escaped us! The recipe had been buried in our copious files for several years before a savvy cook from our committee recognized its merit. You'll like it as much as we . . . great flavors, great colors, and a breeze to prepare. It is most appropriate for fall or winter dinners.

1 leg of lamb
2 cloves garlic, slivered
Salt and coarsely ground pepper
1 large onion, thinly sliced
1 28-ounce can Italian plum tomatoes, undrained
½ teaspoon oregano
½ teaspoon thyme
2 bay leaves
2 cups red burgundy wine

Preheat oven to 450°. Pierce lamb with a small, thin knife to insert garlic slivers throughout. Rub with salt and pepper as desired. Place remaining ingredients, except wine, in a deep roasting pan without a rack. Roast 20 minutes, uncovered. Reduce heat to 350°. Add the 2 cups of wine and bake, un-covered, 1 hour, basting periodically.

½ pound fresh mushrooms, sliced
2 tablespoons butter
2 cups red burgundy wine
6–8 carrots, sliced 1-inch thick on the bias

At end of hour, sauté mushrooms in butter until just soft. Add all to lamb with another 2 cups of wine. Continue roasting 30 more minutes.

In the meantime, steam carrots in a small amount of lightly salted water until tender; about 8–10 minutes. Set aside.

When lamb is done, remove to carving board and cover with foil. Let stand 15 minutes before carving.

Reduce unstrained broth in pan by simmering, uncovered, on top of stove; or by making a paste of 2 tablespoons cornstarch and 2 tablespoons cold water, and stirring into broth until thickened. Fill a warmed tureen with broth and steamed carrots. Accompany it with a big bowl of rice tossed with an abundance of chopped parsley, and buttered petite peas on the side. HERBED CHEESE BREAD would be good with this. Consider SWEDISH RUM PUDDING for dessert.

BARBECUED LEG of LAMB 50

With all of the wonderful freshness of spring and early summer, often the most unpretentious menu is the most appealing.

*Serves
8 to 10*

> 1 7–8 pound leg of lamb, butterflied
> Freshly ground pepper
> Juice of 2 lemons
> 1 large clove garlic, crushed
> 1 generous handful of mint leaves
> Mint sprigs and lemon slices

*Preparation
10 minutes*

*Marinate
6–8 hours*

Place lamb fat side down. If there are some particularly thick sections, make several long, 1-inch deep slashes in them to assist even cooking. Generously sprinkle lamb with pepper and place in a shallow, glass container. Bruise mint leaves with your fingers (isn't that a heavenly experience?!), and combine with lemon juice and garlic. Rub over all of lamb. Cover and let stand at room temperature for 6–8 hours.

*Barbecue
30–45 minutes*

To barbecue, place meat over medium-hot coals, fat-side up, for 30–45 minutes, turning several times with tongs or spatulas.

Let meat rest 10 minutes or so. On a slight diagonal, carve meat in fairly thin slices. Garnish with mint sprigs and lemon slices. Serve with CORN PUDDING, sliced tomatoes sprinkled with seasoned rice vinegar and FINES HERBES, a cucumber salad, and hot SOUR CREAM BISCUITS. If you have our first *Private Collection*, try FRESH BERRIES with ORANGE CREAM for a lovely finish.

51 STEAK SALERA

Serves 4

*Preparation
15 minutes*

*Chill
1–2 hours*

We love this for a hot, summer evening.

1½ pounds top round steak, trimmed of all fat
½ teaspoon ground cumin
1 teaspoon salt
Freshly ground pepper
1 tablespoon oil
1 tablespoon butter

Season meat with cumin, salt, and pepper. In a skillet, over medium-high heat, quickly brown meat on both sides in oil and butter. Reduce heat to medium and cook another 2–3 minutes on each side, until meat is medium-rare. Remove to a shallow, glass dish and chill.

¼ cup olive oil
3 tablespoons lime juice
1 teaspoon dried oregano
2 cloves garlic, crushed
3 tablespoons chopped cilantro (Chinese parsley)
2 tomatoes, sliced
1 avocado, sliced
1 red pepper, sliced in strips or rings
Cilantro sprigs

Slice chilled meat ⅛-inch thick, diagonally across the grain. Combine ¼ cup oil with lime juice, oregano, garlic, and chopped cilantro. Spoon over meat slices and chill 1 hour, periodically turning in marinade.

Place marinated meat slices in center of a chilled, serving platter. Place rows of tomato and avocado slices down each side and decorate with red pepper rings and cilantro sprigs.

CORN PUDDING would be good with this.

Yes! The once lowly flank steak has come into its own. You will be delighted with this recipe for its ease of preparation and yet quite sophisticated flavors. Serve with BROWN BUTTER RICE and a simply prepared green vegetable or MANDARIN SALAD.

Serves 4

Preparation 15 minutes

> 1 tablespoon butter
> 1 tablespoon oil
> 1 1½-pound flank steak
> 3 tablespoons butter
> 3 tablespoons dry vermouth
> 1 tablespoon Dijon mustard
> ¼ teaspoon Worcestershire sauce
> 1½ tablespoons capers
> Watercress

In a 12-inch skillet, melt 1 tablespoon butter with oil over medium heat. Place meat in pan and brown, turning once, about 5–6 minutes, depending on thickness and temperature of the steak. It should be pink in the center when done. Transfer to a carving board and cover with foil to keep warm.

In same pan, over low heat, melt remaining 3 tablespoons butter in pan drippings. With a flat whisk, briskly stir in vermouth, mustard, Worcestershire sauce, and capers. Set aside to keep warm.

At a 45-degree angle, thinly slice meat across the grain. Spoon sauce over all and garnish with watercress.

53 MARINATED BEEF FONDUE

Serves 4

*Preparation
5 minutes*

*Marinate
overnight*

It seems as if years have gone by since beef fondue enjoyed such great popularity. What a shame! It's always fun and so easy to serve. This recipe features a marinade to flavor and tenderize a variety of cuts of meat.

2 pounds sirloin, sirloin tip, or top round
3 tablespoons lemon juice
3 tablespoons vinegar
½ cup oil
1 medium onion, chopped
2 cloves garlic, minced
1 bay leaf
1 teaspoon dry mustard
1½ teaspoons salt
1¼ teaspoons freshly ground pepper
1 cup butter
1 cup peanut oil

Cut meat into 1-inch cubes. Combine remaining ingredients, except butter and peanut oil, and add to meat in a bowl. Cover tightly and refrigerate at least 8 hours (preferably overnight), stirring several times.

When ready to serve, place butter and peanut oil in a 1-quart fondue pot and heat to bubbling, either on top of stove or over fondue burner. Mound raw beef cubes on fondue or dinner plates for your guests to spear and cook in the pot. (Caution them not to eat directly from the hot fondue fork!)

It is customary to serve an assortment of sauces. Since this recipe's marinade provides its own flavors, it is not a requisite, but TARRAGON MUSTARD CREAM is certainly good! To complete your dinner, try MARY LIZ'S SPINACH SALAD and HERBED CHEESE BREAD, followed by CHOCOLATE MOCHA BLITZ TORTE for dessert.

TARRAGON MUSTARD CREAM **54**

A memorable sauce for meats.

2 tablespoons butter, softened
2 tablespoons Dijon mustard
1 tablespoon red wine vinegar
1 teaspoon tarragon vinegar
⅓ cup sour cream
Pinch of cayenne pepper
Salt and coarsely ground pepper
½ teaspoon tarragon leaves

Yield
¾ cup

Preparation
10 minutes

With a whisk, cream together butter and mustard in the top of a double boiler (away from heat). Blend in vinegars and then sour cream. Season with cayenne pepper, and salt and pepper to taste.

Place over hot water and cook slowly, stirring. Do not allow to become too hot. Add tarragon leaves at the last.

55 GRITS SOUFFLÉ

Serves 8

Preparation
15 minutes

Baking
1 hour,
10 minutes

We've tried several popular grits soufflés, but this one is just different enough to make it tops. It's an excellent substitute for potatoes or rice, and holds very well.

1 quart milk
1 cup quick-cooking grits
½ cup butter
1½ teaspoons salt
⅛ teaspoon cayenne pepper
3 generous cups shredded Jarlsberg cheese
6 eggs, well-beaten

Preheat oven to 350°. In a large, heavy saucepan, bring milk just to a boil and stir in grits with a whisk. Reduce heat and continue to stir until it becomes a thick mush; about 3–4 minutes. Remove from heat. Add butter in pieces, salt, cayenne pepper, and cheese, beating in well with a wooden spoon. Beat in eggs.

Pour into a well-buttered, deep, 2½-quart casserole or soufflé dish. Bake, uncovered, for 1 hour and 10 minutes, or until well-puffed and golden brown.

Note: This is an easy recipe to cut in half. Use a 1½-quart soufflé dish and bake 45–50 minutes. If you wish to make this ahead, you may prepare all but the eggs in the morning.

BROWN BUTTER RICE 56

You'll love the rich flavor of the browned butter and the touch of lemon, which makes this most suitable for simply prepared seafood, fish, or chicken.

Serves 4

*Preparation
5 minutes*

*Cooking
20 minutes*

3 cups chicken broth
Juice of 1 lemon
1 cup white, long grain rice
¼ cup butter

Bring chicken broth and lemon juice to a boil in a medium-sized saucepan. Add rice, return to a boil, then reduce heat. Cover and simmer until liquid is absorbed; about 20 minutes.

Over medium heat, melt and simmer butter until it becomes richly browned, but do not burn. Stir into cooked rice. Let sit a few minutes before serving.

APRICOT and PINE NUT PILAF 57

The perfect companion to lamb and pork.

*Serves
4 to 6*

*Preparation
15 minutes*

*Cooking
30 minutes*

1¼ ounces (¼ cup) pine nuts
¼ cup butter
1 onion, chopped
1 cup white, long grain rice
1¾ cups chicken broth
½ cup chopped dried apricots
2 tablespoons butter (optional)

In a large, heavy saucepan, brown pine nuts in butter over medium heat. With slotted spoon, remove nuts and reserve.

Sauté onion in butter until soft, then add rice. Sauté for 1–2 minutes before adding chicken broth. Bring to a boil, reduce heat and simmer, covered, for 20 minutes or until most of stock is absorbed. Add apricots and reserved pine nuts. Cook an additional 10 minutes. Toss with butter just before serving.

58 ITALIAN POTATOES

Serves 6

Preparation
25 minutes

Baking
1 hour,
10 minutes

There is no question that this is a man's recipe, both in origin and appeal. It is just right for barbecues or with hearty meat dishes. It may be prepared ahead, except for the addition of oil.

4 large (or 6 medium) Russet potatoes
½ cup fine, toasted bread crumbs
½ cup freshly grated Parmesan cheese
2–3 large tomatoes, thinly sliced
2 large red onions, thinly sliced
1½ teaspoons oregano
1–1½ teaspoons salt
Freshly ground pepper
½–¾ cup olive oil

Preheat oven to 350°.

Peel and cut potatoes lengthwise into wedges (about 6–8 per potato) and drop into a bowl of cold water.

Combine bread crumbs and grated cheese. Do not dry the wedges before coating them well with the crumb mixture. Place them in a shallow, 9 x 13-inch baking dish, sprinkling any remaining crumbs on top.

Top potatoes with sliced tomatoes and onion rings. Sprinkle with oregano, salt, and a generous grinding of pepper. Drizzle with oil just before baking.

Bake, uncovered, 1 hour and 10 minutes, or until potatoes are brown but still retain some crunchiness.

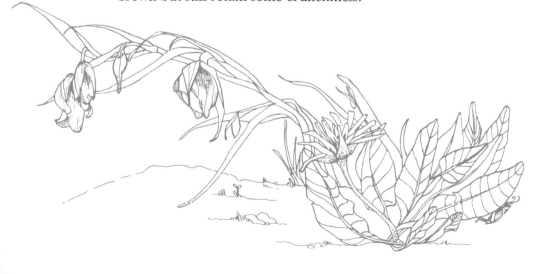

OVEN-FRIED POTATOES

An easy substitute for French fries that you may like even better!

Serves 4

Preparation
15 minutes

Soaking
15 minutes

Baking
30–40
minutes

> 3–4 medium-sized potatoes, unpeeled
> 1/4 cup butter, melted
> 1/2 teaspoon paprika
> Salt to taste

Scrub potatoes and slice as you would large French fries; about 1/2 to 3/4-inch thick. Soak in cold, salted water for 15–30 minutes.

Preheat oven to 450°. Dry potatoes well with paper towels. Toss with melted butter in a 9 x 13-inch baking dish. Spread potatoes out into one layer. Sprinkle with paprika. Bake, uncovered, 30–40 minutes, turning the potatoes several times. When nicely browned, drain on paper towels and sprinkle with salt to taste.

ONIONS in SHERRY

Just the vegetable you've been looking for to serve with grilled steaks.

> 1/4 cup butter
> 5 medium onions, thinly sliced
> 1/2 teaspoon sugar
> 1/2 teaspoon salt
> 1/2 teaspoon freshly ground pepper
> 1/2 cup sherry
> 1/4 cup freshly grated Parmesan cheese
> Dash of nutmeg

Over medium heat, melt butter in a 10-inch skillet. Add onions and season with sugar, salt, and pepper. Cook gently until soft; about 5–8 minutes. Add sherry, increase heat, and cook quickly; about 2–3 minutes. Sprinkle with Parmesan cheese and a dash of nutmeg to serve.

Note: This dish may be prepared ahead and placed in a casserole to reheat in oven.

61 MUSHROOM SOUFFLÉ

Serves 8

Preparation
25 minutes

Baking
40 minutes

This soufflé holds beautifully and mushrooms have never tasted better.

2 pounds mushrooms
½ cup butter
¼ cup butter
¼ cup flour
1 cup light cream
3 eggs, separated
Salt and white pepper to taste

Preheat oven to 350°.

Chop mushrooms, using caps only. Sauté in ½ cup butter for 5 minutes. Drain, reserving juices which should amount to about 1 cup.

In a saucepan, melt ¼ cup butter and stir in flour with a whisk. Cook for a minute, then stir in reserved mushroom broth and light cream. Cook until thickened. Cool and add 1 cup of mixture to sautéed mushrooms. (You will find this yields an extra cup of sauce, but it is difficult to make a smaller amount. Just use the left-over for a heavenly mushroom soup!) At this point, all may be set aside until 50 minutes or so before serving time.

Beat egg yolks until lemon-colored and add to cooled mushroom mixture. Add salt and white pepper to taste, remembering that the following addition of egg whites will reduce the seasoning flavor.

Beat egg whites until stiff and fold into mushroom mixture. Pour into a buttered, 1½-quart soufflé dish. Set in a pan filled with 1–2 inches warm water and bake, uncovered, for 40 minutes or until set. This will hold, thus does not need to be served immediately.

Perfect with roasts, steaks, or simple chicken dishes. We highly recommend it with racks of lamb and LISA'S CARROTS, or ROAST VEAL DIJON from our first *Private Collection*.

Does this stir fond memories? . . . mid-summer . . . fresh tomatoes . . . lazy suppers and long, soft evenings?

Serves
8 to 10

16 ears fresh corn (about 8 cups, cut)
2 teaspoons flour
2 teaspoons sugar
1 teaspoon salt
1⅓ cups milk
4 eggs, beaten
1 tablespoon butter

Preparation
20 minutes

Baking
1 hour

Preheat oven to 300°.

To ensure a delicate dish, use only fresh, raw corn. Thinly slice
the corn from the cob with a very sharp knife, taking care not
to cut too close to the cob. Scrape the cob with the back of
your knife to obtain the best part of all!

Combine dry ingredients with milk. Blend in beaten eggs and
corn. Lavishly grease a shallow, 9 x 13-inch baking dish with
1 tablespoon of butter. Pour in corn mixture. Bake 1 hour or
until top is set.

Note: You may use a deeper baking dish, but increase oven time
accordingly.

63 GINGERED CARROTS

Serves 6

*Preparation
20 minutes*

Perky in flavor and color . . . one of our favorite ways to prepare carrots.

> 7–8 medium carrots
> 1 tablespoon sugar
> 1 teaspoon cornstarch
> ¼ teaspoon salt
> ¼ teaspoon ground ginger
> ¼ cup orange juice
> 2 tablespoons butter
> Chopped parsley

Cut carrots on the bias into ⅛ to ¼-inch thick slices. Cook, covered, in boiling, salted water until just tender; about 7 to 10 minutes. Drain.

Combine sugar, cornstarch, salt, and ginger in a small saucepan. Add orange juice and cook, stirring constantly, until mixture thickens and bubbles. Boil 1 minute then stir in butter. Pour over hot carrots and toss. Garnish with chopped parsley.

Do note that these can be made ahead and reheated without losing any of their zest!

We have seen this recipe elsewhere, but it has been so popular with our committee we could not omit it. Zesty in flavors, it is most suited for barbecue menus or with hearty meats, and may be prepared early in the day.

Serves
4 to 6

Preparation
15 minutes

Baking
15 minutes

8 medium carrots
1 small onion, minced
½ cup mayonnaise
1–2 tablespoons horseradish
½ teaspoon salt
¼ teaspoon freshly ground pepper
1 slice bread
1 tablespoon butter, softened

Preheat oven to 375°.

Slice carrots in thin rounds or julienne. Cook in 1 cup lightly salted water for 5–6 minutes or until tender. Drain, reserving ¼ cup liquid. Place carrots in a buttered, shallow, 1½-quart casserole.

Combine reserved carrot liquid, onion, mayonnaise, horseradish, salt, and pepper. (You may wish to be sparing with the horseradish, depending on its strength.) Spoon over top of carrots.

Generously spread bread with softened butter and sprinkle with a dash or two of paprika. Whirl in a food processor or blender. Sprinkle over top of carrot dish. Bake, uncovered, 15–20 minutes.

65 SWISS CHARD

Serves
4 to 6

Preparation
20 minutes

As simple as its name, this is a very flavorful preparation and loses nothing by being made ahead and reheated. Excellent with seafood.

2 cloves garlic, minced
1 medium onion, sliced
1 tablespoon butter
1 tablespoon oil
2 tomatoes, quartered
6 ounces vegetable or tomato juice
1 bay leaf
1½–2 pounds red or white chard
Salt and freshly ground pepper to taste
Freshly grated Parmesan cheese

In a large saucepan, sauté garlic and onion until soft. Puree tomatoes in a blender with vegetable juice. Add to saucepan with bay leaf and simmer, uncovered, 10–15 minutes.

Wash chard and cut stems into 1-inch pieces. Leave leaves whole. Add stems to tomato sauce and simmer, covered, until tender; about 10 minutes. Add leaves and cook another 5 minutes or until just tender. Add salt and pepper to taste. Serve with a sprinkling of Parmesan cheese.

All those wonderful, natural, simple flavors . . . don't omit anything! You may prepare this dish well-ahead, but do not cook zucchini until just before serving.

Serves 6

Preparation 25 minutes

> 2 pounds zucchini, cubed
> Salt
> 1 medium onion, thinly sliced
> 2 tablespoons oil
> 4 tomatoes, peeled, seeded, and quartered
> 1 green pepper, finely chopped
> 1 clove garlic, minced
> ½ teaspoon salt
> Freshly ground pepper to taste
> 2 tablespoons chopped parsley
> ¼ cup freshly grated Parmesan cheese

Toss cubed zucchini with a little salt and place in a colander to drain. In a 10-inch skillet, sauté onion in oil until golden. Add tomatoes, green pepper, and garlic. Season with salt and pepper, and simmer over low heat for 15 minutes.

Add zucchini, cover, and simmer until tender; about 3–5 minutes. Before serving, sprinkle with freshly chopped parsley and Parmesan cheese.

67 HERBED CHERRY TOMATOES

Serves 8

*Preparation
20 minutes*

The simplicity and the fact that it may be prepared ahead make this a popular recipe. Excellent with grilled meats, ONIONS IN SHERRY, and fresh asparagus or broccoli.

36–48 firm cherry tomatoes
2–3 tablespoons butter
4 tablespoons chopped fresh herbs
    (all or some: parsley, chives, tarragon, chervil)
Salt and freshly ground pepper

A handful at a time, drop tomatoes into a saucepan of boiling water and boil 3–4 seconds; just enough to loosen skins. Remove with a slotted spoon. Using a small, sharp-pointed knife, remove stems and slip off skins. Place tomatoes in one layer in a non-aluminum container. Cover and refrigerate.

Just before serving, heat butter to bubbling in a large skillet. Add tomatoes, herbs, and seasonings. Gently shake pan to roll tomatoes in butter until heated through. Turn into a warm serving dish or use to garnish your meat or vegetable platter.

68 SICILIAN BROCCOLI

*Serves
4 to 6*

*Preparation
10 minutes*

You will be so pleased by how good this simple dish is!

1½–2 pounds broccoli
¼ pound butter
1 clove garlic, minced
½ teaspoon anchovy paste
Juice of 1 lemon
Salt and pepper to taste

Steam the broccoli until crisp-tender. In a small saucepan, melt butter over medium-low heat, adding garlic and anchovy paste. Blend with a whisk and let gently simmer for a minute or two. Add lemon juice, salt and pepper. Pour over cooked broccoli.

One of the prettiest vegetable dishes one can imagine, it doubles as a garnish for meat, chicken, or fish platters. Easily prepared ahead.

Serves 10

*Preparation
20 minutes*

*Baking
10 minutes
(optional)*

> 10 medium tomatoes
> 1 bunch broccoli (1¼ pounds)
> 1 small onion, chopped
> 4 tablespoons butter
> ⅛ teaspoon allspice
> ½ cup cream (optional)
> Salt and freshly ground pepper

With a small, sharp knife, carefully remove stems, cutting as little of the tomato as possible, for appearance's sake. With a larger knife, cut tomatoes in half *lengthwise* (from stem to bottom). Remove pulp, leaving ¼ to ½-inch thick shells. Turn upside down on paper toweling to drain.

Cut broccoli into large florets. Cut stems into 1-inch lengths. Lightly salt and cook, covered, in 2 inches of boiling water until just tender; about 6–8 minutes. Drain immediately and rinse in cold water to maintain color.

In a small skillet, sauté onion in butter until tender. Sprinkle with allspice. Add cream (but if you are calorie conscious, you may omit or substitute milk) and simmer for a minute or two. Puree with broccoli in a blender, processing in batches. Add salt and pepper to taste. At this point, you may cover and set puree aside until close to serving time.

Shortly before serving, the puree may be warmed in top of a double boiler then spooned into raw tomato shells and served as is. Or place filled tomatoes in a lightly buttered baking dish and bake, uncovered, at 350° for 10 minutes; just long enough to heat through.

Serves 6

*Preparation
30 minutes*

*Marinate
1–2 hours*

So appealing to the eye, use it as a vegetable dish or salad when you are looking for a special touch.

½ pound whole baby carrots*
2 teaspoons sugar
½ teaspoon salt
½ pound whole, fresh, green beans
2 teaspoons salt

*If baby carrots are not available, buy the youngest you can find, then peel and cut into 1½-inch long sticks.

Place the carrots in a saucepan along with sugar, ½ teaspoon salt, and just enough water to cover. With lid on, simmer until barely tender; about 5–7 minutes. Drain.

Cook beans in 2 quarts boiling water with 2 teaspoons salt, until crisp-tender; about 5 minutes. To preserve their fresh, green color, drain and rinse immediately in cold water until chilled through.

¼ cup olive oil
1 tablespoon tarragon vinegar
¼ teaspoon dry mustard
1 tablespoon chopped chives
2 teaspoons chopped, fresh thyme or tarragon
  (½ teaspoon dried)
2 teaspoons chopped, fresh chervil
  (½ teaspoon dried)
1 clove garlic, minced
Salt (optional)
⅛ teaspoon ground white pepper

Combine above ingredients with a whisk until well-blended. Pour over vegetables and marinate, covered, at room temperature for 1–2 hours (or 6 hours, chilled). The flavors are best when served at room temperature.

If you have just plucked the squash from the vine, you may wish to marinate it only an hour at room temperature to preserve the fresh quality, but overnight will please you, too. This is a tasty substitute for the ubiquitous, tossed green salad at summer barbecues.

Serves 8

Preparation 15 minutes

Marinate 1–24 hours

4 small zucchini
4 small yellow squash
½ cup chopped celery (optional)
1 red onion, finely chopped (optional)
1 red bell pepper (optional)
1 cup sherry wine vinegar
½ cup sugar
⅓ cup olive oil
1 teaspoon salt
1 teaspoon freshly ground pepper

Slice the zucchini and yellow squash, paper-thin, into a large, shallow bowl. Add celery, red onion, and bell pepper, if you wish (although the squash is delicious on its own).

Combine remaining ingredients in a saucepan. Bring to a boil to dissolve sugar. Pour over vegetables while still hot. Cover and marinate at room temperature or chill overnight. Drain and serve.

72 RAW MUSHROOMS in MUSTARD CREAM

Serves
6 to 8

Preparation
15 minutes

The delicate quality of the mushrooms is enhanced by the creamy sauce . . . an excellent first course or companion to grilled steaks, a simple tossed green salad, and HERBED CHEESE BREAD.

    2 tablespoons tarragon vinegar
    2 tablespoons Dijon mustard
    ¼ teaspoon Worcestershire sauce
    1 teaspoon sugar
    ½ teaspoon salt
    ½ teaspoon ground white pepper
    1 egg
    ½ cup oil
    3 tablespoons heavy cream
    ½ pound large mushrooms, sliced
    Chopped parsley and watercress

In a small bowl, combine vinegar, mustard, Worcestershire sauce, sugar, salt, and white pepper.

In an electric blender, blend egg at high speed until light-colored. Add oil in a slow, steady stream. Add mustard-vinegar mixture and blend. Pour into a medium-size bowl, and beat in cream with a whisk or electric beater. If not serving immediately, chill.

To serve, divide mushroom slices among small, individual plates. Pour sauce over and dust with chopped parsley. Add a sprig of watercress.

Very good and very pretty . . . the perfect salad to take along to a barbecue or tailgate party. It may be prepared some hours ahead and chilled.

1–1½ pounds broccoli
1 head cauliflower
2 small zucchini, sliced
2 baskets cherry tomatoes, trimmed
½ pound mushrooms, halved
2 bunches green onions, chopped
1 cup diced celery
2 8-ounce cans sliced water chestnuts, drained
1 6-ounce can pitted ripe olives, drained
2 cups diced Swiss or Fontina cheese

Cut small florets from broccoli and cauliflower. Combine with remaining ingredients and toss with the following dressing.

2 cups mayonnaise
2 tablespoons horseradish
2 tablespoons lemon juice
1–2 tablespoons tarragon vinegar
1 tablespoon dry mustard
2 cloves garlic, minced
Salt to taste
Chopped parsley

Combine the above ingredients except parsley. Toss with vegetables and cheese and place in a large glass bowl for a pretty effect. Before serving, sprinkle with chopped parsley.

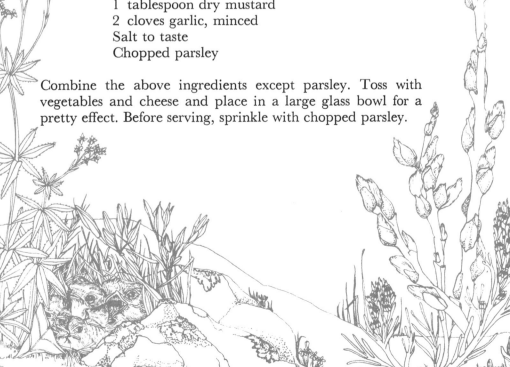

74 MANDARIN ORANGE SALAD

Serves 6

*Preparation
15 minutes*

This appealing salad can be served in a bowl or attractively arranged on a platter or individual plates.

2 heads red lettuce (or 3 heads butter)
½ cup chopped celery
⅓ cup chopped green onions
½ cup watercress sprigs
¼ cup chopped parsley
1 11-ounce can mandarin oranges, drained
½ cup chopped walnuts, almonds, or pecans

Dress with the following just before serving.

½ cup olive oil
¼ cup tarragon vinegar
2 tablespoons sugar
½ teaspoon Worcestershire sauce
1 teaspoon salt
Freshly ground pepper to taste
Dash of Tabasco sauce (optional)

With a whisk, blend the above ingredients thoroughly until sugar is dissolved.

Note: Delicious substitutions are grapefruit and avocado slices in place of the mandarin oranges, and pine nuts instead of walnuts.

ENDIVE and WATERCRESS SALAD 75

A refreshing salad that lets understatement be the key to a successful menu. If kumquats are in season, their tang and the crunchiness of the frozen walnuts lend special touches.

Serves 6

Preparation 20 minutes

> 6 small, tight Belgian endives
> 3 bunches watercress, washed and trimmed to bite-size
> 6 green onions, chopped
> 18–24 fresh kumquats, sliced ¼-inch thick and seeded (optional)
> ¾ cup coarsely chopped walnuts, frozen

If preparing for individual salads, quarter endives lengthwise. Arrange on top of beds of watercress, sprinkling with chopped onion, sliced kumquats, and frozen walnuts, then drizzling with dressing. For a salad bowl, slice endives crosswise, ½-inch thick. Toss with remaining ingredients.

DRESSING

> 2 tablespoons white wine vinegar
> 1 teaspoon Dijon mustard
> ¼ teaspoon salt
> Freshly ground pepper to taste
> ½ cup olive oil

With a whisk, blend vinegar, mustard, salt, and pepper. Add oil gradually, beating constantly with a whisk.

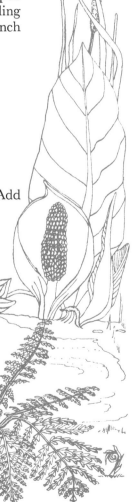

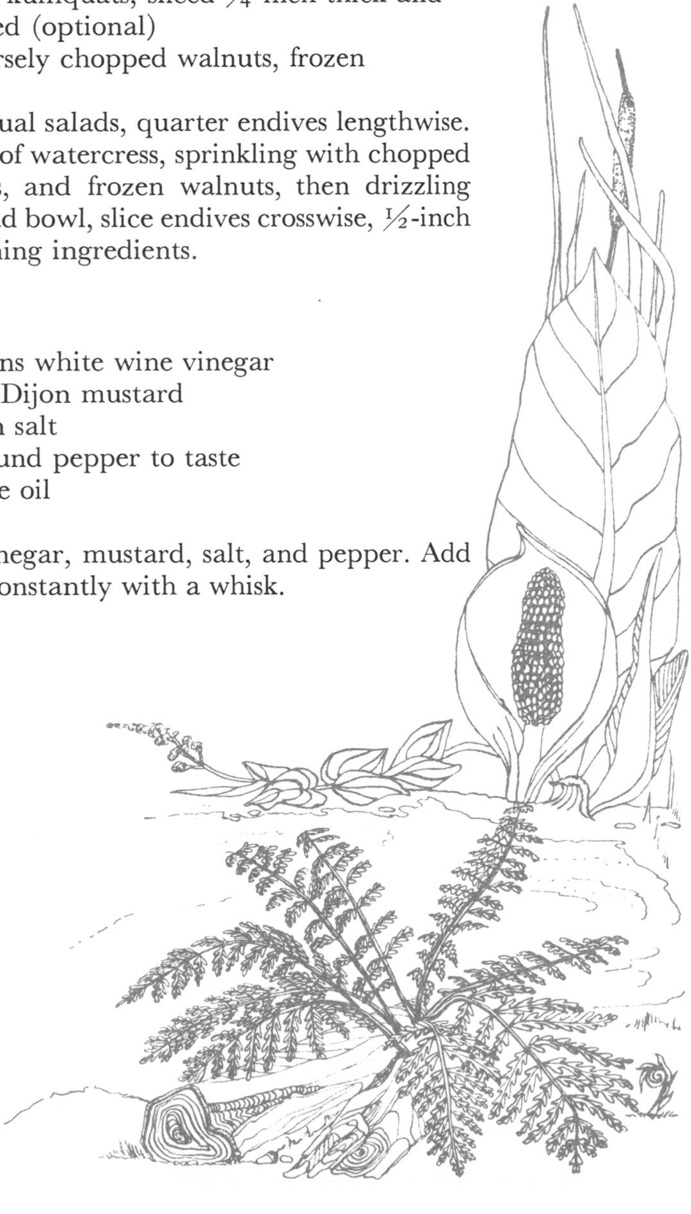

The crisp, cold lettuce with cheese and the savory, hot mush-rooms do wonderful things for each other. Serve as a first course or with your entree . . . particularly steaks or roast beef.

2 heads Bibb or butter lettuce
4 ounces (1 cup) shredded Monterey jack cheese
2 tablespoons butter
½ pound mushrooms, sliced
12 cocktail onions, chilled
Freshly ground black pepper

Wash and dry lettuce. Put in a bowl along with shredded cheese; cover and refrigerate. Place 4 salad plates in refrigerator or freezer to chill.

Just before serving, heat butter in skillet and sauté mushrooms until just soft; about 3–4 minutes.

Toss lettuce and cheese with desired amount of dressing (see below). Divide among chilled plates, garnishing each with 3 cocktail onions. Top salad with piping hot mushrooms. Add a good grinding of black pepper and serve immediately.

DRESSING

½ cup olive oil
¼ cup white wine vinegar
2 tablespoons Dijon mustard
2–3 large cloves garlic
¼ teaspoon salt

Combine above ingredients in blender and whir at high speed. Set aside until serving time.

There is an excellent spinach salad in our first *Private Collection,* but this one received so many plaudits it couldn't be forgotten.

1 bunch spinach (¾–1 pound)
5–6 slices bacon, cut in slivers
3 tablespoons bacon drippings
2 tablespoons orange juice
2 tablespoons cider vinegar
2 tablespoons currant jelly
⅓–½ cup sliced almonds, toasted

Rinse, trim, and dry spinach. Tear into bite-sized pieces in a salad bowl. Fry bacon until crisp. Drain on paper toweling, reserving 3 tablespoons of the drippings in pan. Add orange juice, vinegar, and jelly to skillet. Just before serving, bring to a boil and pour over spinach. Toss with bacon and toasted almonds.

78 MUSTARD ASPIC

Serves
10 to 12

Preparation
25 minutes

Chill
2–3 hours

Use your prettiest mold for this delicate accompaniment to ham, pork, or tongue.

1 packet unflavored gelatin
½ cup sugar
2 teaspoons dry mustard
1 teaspoon salt
¼ cup white wine vinegar with tarragon
¼ cup white vinegar
½ cup boiling water
1 tablespoon Dijon mustard
3 eggs, lightly beaten
1 cup heavy cream, whipped

Combine gelatin with dry ingredients in top of double boiler and place over boiling water. With a whisk, add vinegars, boiling water, and Dijon mustard. Continuing to beat with a whisk, add eggs. Beat until frothy and thickened like heavy cream. Cool. (If you wish, set over a bowl of ice and stir with a whisk until room temperature.)

Whisk cooled egg mixture into whipped cream and pour into a well-oiled, 4-cup mold. Chill until set. Unmold onto a pretty serving plate and decorate with watercress or parsley sprigs.

Note: Sprinkle generously with chopped fresh dill or dried dill weed and serve with thin slices of cold, leftover lamb. Super!

As you well know, just the right touch of herbs can eliminate *Yield* the convenient salt shaker and turn a soup, a salad, a meat or *1 ounce* vegetable dish, into an epicurean experience. A tale is told that two diligent souls, with tweezers in hand, sorted a pot of "herbs from Provence" to determine the exact varieties and quantities of this famous blend. Supposedly, down to the very last fennel seed, this is the recipe. You can have such fun filling your own little pots or pouches for hostess or holiday gifts.

> 3 tablespoons dried marjoram
> 3 tablespoons dried summer savory
> 3 tablespoons dried thyme
> 1 tablespoon dried sweet basil
> 1½ teaspoons dried rosemary
> ½ teaspoon crushed sage
> ½ teaspoon fennel seeds
> 3–4 pinches lavender

Combine, mix well, and store in an air-tight container.

Note: To create an outstanding HERB CHEESE, combine 8 ounces each of cream and feta cheeses in a food processor, along with a little pressed garlic, a tablespoon or so of cream, freshly ground pepper, and FINES HERBES to taste (we suggest at least a tablespoon).

80 HERBED CHEESE BREAD

Serves 8

Preparation
15 minutes

Baking
30 minutes

You probably can guess how good this is! Because it is rich, serve it with simple foods such as steaks, salads, or hearty, vegetable soups.

> 1 round loaf sourdough or French bread
> ½ cup butter
> 1 tablespoon chopped parsley
> 1 teaspoon minced onion
> 1 teaspoon poppy seeds
> ½ pound Monterey jack cheese, sliced

Preheat oven to 350°.

Cut loaf into 1½-inch squares or diamonds, leaving bottom crust intact.

In a small saucepan, melt butter with parsley, onion, and poppy seeds. Dribble over openings in bread then insert a cheese slice in each one. Wrap in foil. (Bread may be set aside at this time.)

Place on baking sheet and bake 15 minutes. Loosen foil to expose top and bake another 15 minutes to lightly brown. Serve while hot.

The rye flour gives this a marvelous nutty quality. It's great for barbecues, with hearty stews, or at breakfast time with sausage.

Serves 6

Preparation 10 minutes

Baking 20 minutes

> ¾ cup white flour, unsifted
> ¾ cup rye flour, unsifted
> ½ cup cornmeal
> 3 teaspoons baking powder
> Pinch of salt
> 2 eggs
> ½ cup sugar
> ½ cup melted butter
> 1 cup milk

Preheat oven to 425°.

Combine all dry ingredients except sugar. In a medium-large bowl, beat together eggs and sugar, then add melted butter. With a wooden spoon, mix in dry ingredients, alternating with milk.

Pour into a greased, 9-inch square baking dish. Bake 20 minutes.

82 SOUR CREAM BISCUITS

Yield 16

Preparation 10 minutes

Baking 10–12 minutes

Not only are these biscuits cloud-like, they are versatile,* and they may be made hours ahead of time, covered and refrigerated until baking.

2 cups unbleached flour
4 teaspoons baking powder
½ teaspoon salt
½ teaspoon cream of tartar
2 teaspoons sugar
½ cup vegetable shortening
⅓ cup sour cream
⅓ cup milk

Sift together dry ingredients into a large bowl. Cut in shortening until mixture resembles coarse crumbs. Add sour cream and milk all at once. Stir with a fork only dough follows it around bowl.

Turn dough out onto a floured board. Lightly knead for only a few seconds. The secret is to handle the dough as gently as you would a baby!

Pat or roll dough out to ½-inch thickness. Cut with a biscuit cutter and place on an ungreased cookie sheet. At this point, you may refrigerate until baking time.

Preheat oven to 450°. Bake 10–12 minutes.

*Note: You may use the dough to make one great, big, beautiful SHORTCAKE by increasing the sugar to 1½ tablespoons. Make HERB BISCUITS to top a stew such as RAGOUT OF PORK by adding 2 teaspoons chopped parsley and ½ teaspoon dried summer savory to the dry ingredients.

This truly is "homemade" bread . . . just what you would picture; great, big, beautiful loaves of snowy white bread with golden brown crusts. We don't know what the secret is, but the recipe is very easy to make and guarantees success every time. There is no kneading and the time is not critical. You may cut the recipe in half, but we'll wager that you'll wish you hadn't!

Yield
4 loaves

Preparation
15 minutes

Risings
1 hour
2–4 hours
1 hour

Baking
45 minutes

    2 packages dry yeast
    2 tablespoons sugar
    ½ cup lukewarm water
    1 cup powdered non-fat milk
    4 cups unbleached flour
    4 cups lukewarm water
    ½ cup sugar
    ⅓ cup oil
    5 teaspoons salt
    8 cups unbleached flour

Combine yeast, sugar, and lukewarm water in a small bowl. Let sit until it foams; about 10 minutes.

In a very large bowl, put powdered milk, 4 cups flour, and 4 cups lukewarm water. Add yeast mixture. Stir with a sturdy, wooden spoon until well-blended. Cover and let sit in a warm place for 1 hour.

Add remaining ingredients and mix well. Cover and let sit until double in bulk; between 2 and 4 hours.

Turn out onto a well-floured board and divide into 4 parts. (Dough will be sticky.) Shape each part into a loaf, working out any air bubbles. Put into 4 greased, 9 x 5-inch, loaf pans. Cover and let sit until double; about 1 hour.

Bake at 350° for 45 minutes. Remove bread from pans and cool on racks.

84 HOOTSLA

Serves 4

*Preparation
15 minutes*

We couldn't resist including this Pennsylvania Dutch version of French toast that somehow (thankfully!) found its way to the West Coast. Warm applesauce and sausage are musts with this.

½ loaf day-old sourdough or French bread
½ cup butter
3 eggs
½ cup milk
Salt and pepper to taste

Cut bread, crust and all, into cubes. Melt butter in a large, heavy skillet. Add bread cubes and brown, stirring. Beat eggs until light-colored, then combine with milk, salt and pepper. Remove bread from heat. Pour egg/milk mixture over bread then return to heat and stir constantly until egg is entirely cooked.

Serve at once with cinnamon-sugar or warm maple syrup.

For that very special late breakfast . . . midnight or otherwise!

*Serves
2 to 4*

*Preparation
15 minutes*

6 eggs, separated
2–2½ tablespoons powdered sugar
⅓ cup orange juice
1 tablespoon grated orange rind
⅛ teaspoon salt
2 tablespoons unsalted butter
Sugar
Mint sprigs and orange slices

Preheat broiler, placing rack 6–8 inches below.

Beat egg yolks until lemon-colored. Beat in powdered sugar, orange juice, and rind. In a large bowl, beat egg whites with salt until peaks form. Fold a spoonful of whites into yolk mixture, then gently but thoroughly fold latter into rest of egg whites.

Melt butter in a 10-inch skillet over medium-high heat, tipping pan to coat sides. When it begins to sizzle, pour in blended eggs and reduce heat to medium. Cook 3–5 minutes, until nicely browned on bottom and the top has just set. Place under broiler and watch closely. When top of omelet begins to brown, turn broiler off and shut oven door. Let sit for 5 minutes.

Slide omelet out (or invert) onto a warm platter. Sprinkle lightly with sugar, and garnish with mint sprigs and orange slices. Serve with crisp bacon and buttered scones . . . strawberries and champagne?

86 SOUR CREAM COFFEE CAKE

Serves 12

Preparation 20 minutes

Baking 1 hour

The lightest and loveliest of all the coffee cakes we have tested. The secret is in the proportions of the ingredients, and cake flour is a must.

½ pound butter, softened
2 cups sugar
2 eggs
½ teaspoon vanilla
1 cup sour cream
1¾ cups sifted cake flour
1 teaspoon baking powder
¼ teaspoon salt
½ cup chopped pecans or walnuts
2 tablespoons dark brown sugar
1½ teaspoons cinnamon

Preheat oven to 350°. Generously butter a 10-inch tube pan.

In a large mixing bowl, cream together butter and sugar. Add eggs, one at a time, beating well after each addition; then add vanilla and sour cream. Sift together cake flour, baking powder, and salt. Stir into sour cream mixture.

Combine nuts, brown sugar, and cinnamon. Spoon half of batter into prepared tube pan. Sprinkle with half of nut mixture. Cover with rest of batter and then remaining nut mixture.

Bake 1 hour. Cool in pan on rack. When completely cool, carefully remove cake from pan so that it can be displayed, topping-end up, on cake plate.

Serve as a coffee or teatime treat, or with a gorgeous fruit salad. Dress it up for a dinner party by splitting and filling with a custard cream, then drizzling with chocolate sauce.

Serves 12

*Soaking
1 hour*

⅔–1 cup poppy seeds
(two 2-ounce or 2¾-ounce jars)
1 cup milk

*Preparation
20 minutes*

The amount of poppy seeds that one uses is a matter of taste. Combine seeds and milk in a small saucepan. Bring to a boil, remove from heat, and let stand 1 hour.

*Baking
50 minutes*

1 cup butter, softened
1⅔ cups sugar
3 egg yolks
2 cups sifted flour
2½ teaspoons baking powder
½ teaspoon salt
3 egg whites
2 teaspoons vanilla
Powdered sugar

Preheat oven to 350°. Butter and flour a 10-inch bundt pan.

Cream together butter and sugar. Beat in egg yolks, one at a time. Beat in poppy seed milk.

Sift together flour, baking powder, and salt. Using a rubber spatula, stir dry ingredients into creamed mixture. Beat egg whites until stiff but not dry. Gently fold into batter with vanilla.

Pour batter into prepared bundt pan. Bake 50 minutes or until cake just begins to leave sides. Cool on a rack for 10 minutes then invert onto cake plate. When cool, sift powdered sugar over top.

88 LEMON DAINTY

Serves 6

Preparation
15 minutes

Baking
1 hour

This was found, neatly penned, on a tattered page of an old, family recipe book. The date was 1931, the description: ". . . a delicate crust will form on top of the pudding . . . supplies its own sauce. Very fine." It is a very fine pudding cake . . . pretty, simple, and refreshing.

> 1 cup sugar
> ¼ cup flour
> ⅛ teaspoon salt
> 2 tablespoons butter, melted
> 5–6 tablespoons lemon juice
> Grated rind of 2 small lemons
> 3 egg yolks
> 1½ cups milk
> 3 egg whites

Preheat oven to 350°.

Combine dry ingredients in a large mixing bowl. Add melted butter, lemon juice, and rind. Blend with a whisk. Add yolks and milk, and beat with whisk until well-blended.

Beat whites until stiff but not dry. Fold into lemon mixture. Pour into a greased, 1½-quart, soufflé dish. Set dish in a shallow roasting pan filled with 1 inch of hot water. Bake 1 hour.

This suits almost any menu and may be served hot or cold in shallow bowls. It is lovely with fresh berries.

A light, refreshing dessert of fine consistency . . . lovely with berries and mint.

*Serves
6 to 8*

⅓ cup fresh lime juice (2–3 limes)
1 teaspoon flour
3 eggs
1½ cups sugar
¼ teaspoon salt
1 cup boiling water
1 tablespoon grated lime rind
1 egg white, beaten
1 cup heavy cream, beaten
Tiny mint sprigs

*Preparation
30 minutes*

Chill

Combine lime juice and flour. In a large saucepan, whisk together 3 eggs, sugar, and salt until light-colored. Add lime juice/flour mixture, then boiling water, continuing to beat briskly with a whisk. Place over medium heat and continue to stir until it thickens slightly and *just* begins to boil. Remove from heat.

Chill in refrigerator, stirring periodically, or set over a bowl of ice and whisk until cold. Fold in grated lime rind, beaten egg white, and whipped cream, blending gently but thoroughly. Chill until serving time.

Serve in pretty, stemmed glasses with tiny sprigs of mint, and CHOCOLATE WAFERS at the side; or in shallow, glass bowls with sugared fresh raspberries.

90 LEMON PIE

Serves 8

Preparation
10 minutes
15 minutes

Cooling

Baking
5 minutes

Here is a very easy and different approach to a beautiful, classic dessert. We think you'll love it, and the pie crust is superb (for quiches, too).

PIE CRUST

1½ cups flour
¾ teaspoon salt
⅔ cup vegetable shortening
3 tablespoons cold water

Preheat oven to 450°.

Sift together flour and salt into a mixing bowl. Remove ¼-cup of the flour mixture to a small bowl. Cut shortening into first bowl, using a pastry cutter or knives, until size of small peas. With a fork, combine cold water and reserved ¼-cup flour until a smooth paste. Stir into shortening and flour, combining well.

Because this is a very tender pastry, it's best to use a pastry cloth and rolling pin cover. Roll out to ⅛-inch thickness to line a 9-inch glass pie plate (there will be some excess). Be careful not to over-stretch dough, since it can cause shrinkage while baking.

Fold dough in half, then half again, to transfer to pie plate. Unfold and gently press into dish, crimping edges of pastry securely to rim. Press out any air bubbles under pastry. Use a table fork to prick throughout, including sides. (The latter is done only for pie shells that are to be pre-baked.)

Bake 8–10 minutes, until very lightly browned. Cool on rack.

LEMON FILLING

4 egg yolks
½ cup sugar
1 tablespoon water
Juice and grated rind of 1 lemon
4 egg whites
½ cup sugar

Reduce oven tempeature to 400°.

In top of double boiler (away from heat), beat egg yolks with sugar until light in color. Add water, lemon juice, and rind. Place over boiling water and stir constantly with a whisk until thick; about 3–5 minutes. Remove and cool, stirring constantly. (A speedy method would be to place bowl over a bowl of ice.)

In a separate bowl, beat egg whites until they form soft mounds. Gradually beat in sugar. Continue beating until stiff peaks are formed.

Blend half of beaten egg whites into cooled lemon mixture. Pour into baked, cooled pie shell. Gently spread rest of meringue over top, making sure it touches crust everywhere to prevent shrinkage. Swirl into pretty peaks.

Bake until meringue is lightly browned; about 5 minutes. Cool on a rack. The pie may sit out on counter for up to 2 hours before serving. If any longer, refrigerate.

91 BLUEBERRY SHERBET in MERINGUES

Serves 12

Preparation
30 minutes

Baking
40 minutes

Freeze

"The rich flavor of blueberries is so pronounced in this sherbet that people tend to eat it slowly. They want the good taste to last . . . and last . . . and last."—Jane Benet, food editor of the *San Francisco Chronicle*.

Blueberry lovers, everywhere . . . here is the ultimate dessert!

> 2 cups blueberries (or 1 10-ounce package
>   frozen, without sugar)
> ½ cup sugar
> ½ cup water
> 1 tablespoon unflavored gelatin
> ¼ cup lemon juice
> 2 cups heavy cream

Combine blueberries, sugar, and water in a saucepan. Simmer 10 minutes. Soak gelatin in lemon juice, then stir into hot blueberries. Chill until slightly thickened.

Whip cream until soft peaks form, then fold in blueberry mixture. Cover and freeze at least 3 hours.

Remove from freezer 30 minutes before serving. Scoop sherbet into meringue shells and serve at once. BLUEBERRY KIR SAUCE is spectacular with this!

> 6 egg whites
> ¼ teaspoon salt
> 2 cups sugar
> ½ teaspoon anise flavoring (optional)

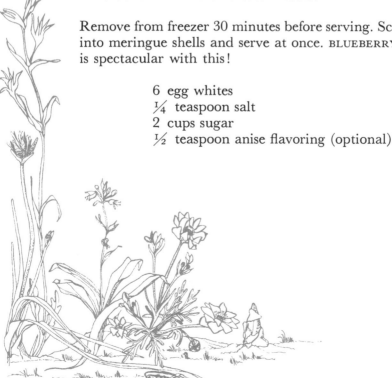

Preheat oven to 275°. Oil 2 foil-lined cookie sheets or cover sheets with parchment paper.

Beat egg whites and salt until stiff. Beat in sugar very gradually, continuing to beat until mixture is stiff and glossy.

Create 6 meringue shells per sheet by using a pastry bag, fitted with a 1-inch star tip, or by spreading a small spoonful of meringue into a 3 to 4-inch circle, then using a spoon and additional meringue to build up edge. Bake 40 minutes or until completely dry. Let cool in oven.

SOUR CREAM ICE CREAM 92

If you are fortunate enough to have an ice cream maker, all the better, but this will be just as wonderful without it.

Serves
6 to 8

Preparation
10 minutes

Freeze

    4 large eggs
    1 cup sugar
    4 teaspoons vanilla
    4 cups sour cream

Beat eggs and sugar until latter is *completely* dissolved. Add vanilla and sour cream.

If not processing in an ice cream maker, tightly cover and freeze until half-frozen. Whirl in a food processor or blender. Pour into a pretty mold, if you wish. Press plastic film across surface, then tightly seal with a lid or foil. Freeze.

Remove from freezer 20–30 minutes before serving. At dessert time, unmold onto platter or scoop into individual bowls. Serve with fresh berries or ORANGE WINE SAUCE or BLUEBERRY KIR SAUCE. CHOCOLATE WAFERS would be appropriate.

93 BLUEBERRY KIR SAUCE

Serves
6 to 8

Yield
2 cups

Preparation
10 minutes

Chill

The sauce keeps beautifully in the refrigerator, so that it is readily at hand to guarantee a pretty, last-minute dessert. It's the finishing touch for BLUEBERRY SHERBET.

½ cup Crème de Cassis (black currant liqueur)
1 tablespoon cornstarch
¾ cup dry white wine
1 tablespoon lemon juice
1 tablespoon butter
1½ cups fresh or frozen blueberries

In a bowl, whisk together Cassis and cornstarch, then add wine and lemon juice.

Melt butter in a medium-sized saucepan and stir in Cassis mixture. Over medium heat, continue stirring until thick and glossy, then add berries. Stir until they burst. Chill.

94 ORANGE WINE SAUCE

Serves
6 to 8

Yield
2 cups

Preparation
10 minutes

Chill

Sauces such as this and BLUEBERRY KIR SAUCE are perfect for the spur-of-the-moment dinner party. They take only a few minutes to make and can be served over ice cream or cheese cake, plus they keep well in the refrigerator. This one is excellent over orange sherbet.

½ cup sugar
1 tablespoon cornstarch
½ cup orange juice
1 tablespoon grated orange rind
½ cup sherry
1 tablespoon lemon juice
1 cup diced fresh orange slices (or mandarin orange segments)

Combine sugar, cornstarch, orange juice, grated rind, and sherry in a small saucepan. Blend well with a whisk and cook over medium heat, stirring until sauce thickens and becomes clear. Remove from heat, and add lemon juice and diced oranges. Chill before serving.

Just as pretty as they can be . . . particularly if you dress them with candied violets.

Serves
10 to 12

Preparation
40 minutes

Chill
8 hours

 10 large temple or navel oranges
 ¾ cup grated orange rind
 1½ cups sugar
 1½ cups light Karo syrup
 4–5 drops red food coloring
 1½ cups water
 ¼ cup lemon juice
 ¼ cup Grand Marnier or Triple Sec liqueur

Grate rind of oranges to attain ¾ cup. Peel oranges, removing pith and membrane. Cut in thin slices into a glass bowl.

In a saucepan, combine sugar, Karo syrup, food coloring, and water. Bring to a boil, stirring *only* until sugar is dissolved. Simmer, uncovered, for 10 minutes. Add grated rind and continue cooking until syrup is slightly thickened; about 20–30 minutes. Remove from heat and stir in lemon juice and liqueur. Cool and pour over oranges. Chill 8 hours, turning oranges in syrup occasionally.

 4 egg yolks
 2 tablespoons sugar
 ¼ cup Grand Marnier liqueur
 ⅓ cup heavy cream, whipped

In top of double boiler (away from heat), beat egg yolks until thick. Gradually add sugar, beating until fluffy and light in color and mixture forms soft peaks. Place over simmering water. Slowly add liqueur, continuing to beat until mixture forms soft mounds; about 5 minutes. Set top of boiler in a bowl of ice and continue beating until cool. Gently fold in whipped cream. Refrigerate until serving.

Serve orange slices in their syrup in a pretty glass bowl. Top, if possible, with candied violets. Pass sauce separately.

96 COCONUT MOLD with BRANDIED PRUNES

Serves
6 to 8

Preparation
30 minutes

Chill
3 hours

Delicious and certainly unusual, this provides a dramatic finish to unique dinners such as BEBE'S CHICKEN CURRY and FEIJOADA COMPLETA. The color contrasts are smashing! If possible, use fresh coconut for special quality.

> 2 cups shredded coconut meat
>   (1 medium coconut)*
> 1½ tablespoons unflavored gelatin
> 1½ cups coconut milk (if unavailable, see index)
> ¾ cup sugar
> ¼ teaspoon salt
> 1 cup heavy cream
> 1 teaspoon vanilla
> Mint sprigs

*If using fresh coconut, pierce 2 of the 3 eyes of a coconut, using an ice pick and hammer. Drain, reserving milk. Roast at 400° for 20 minutes or freeze at 0° for 1 hour. Wrap in a towel and pound with a hammer to break shell. Remove shell and pare away brown skin. Grate or shred coconut to obtain 2 cups (a food processor does a good job).

Dissolve gelatin in a ½ cup of the coconut milk in a medium-sized bowl. Heat remaining 1 cup coconut milk with sugar and salt. Stir into gelatin. Chill in refrigerator or stir with a whisk over a bowl of ice until it begins to thicken. Whip cream until soft peaks form and fold into gelatin mixture with coconut meat and vanilla. Pour into an oiled, 5–6 cup mold (a melon mold is most attractive), and chill at least 3 hours.**

When ready to serve, unmold into a shallow serving dish and surround with BRANDIED PRUNES and mint sprigs.

> 1 12-ounce package dried, pitted prunes (2 cups)
> 2½ cups water
> ¼ cup brown sugar
> 1 tablespoon lemon juice
> 2–4 tablespoons Cointreau liqueur

In a medium saucepan, bring prunes and water to a boil and simmer 1–2 minutes. Remove from heat and let stand 1 hour. With a slotted spoon, remove plumped prunes to a bowl. Add brown sugar to liquid and simmer 3–5 minutes, or until reduced to half. Remove from heat. Add lemon juice, 2 tablespoons Cointreau, and prunes. Serve at room temperature, adding 2 more tablespoons of Cointreau if you wish.

**Note:* For a more informal dinner, the dessert does not need to be molded. Just chill in a bowl until well-set, then spoon into shallow glass bowls and surround with the prunes and their sauce. Decorate with sprigs of mint.

DAN'S PERSIMMON DESSERT 97

Nothing could be quicker or tastier . . . serve with MOLASSES CRISPS.

Serves 4

> 2 large, very ripe persimmons, peeled
> 3 ounces Cointreau
> 1 pint ice cream

*Preparation
5 minutes*

Whir persimmons, Cointreau, and half of ice cream in a blender. Divide remaining ice cream between 4 large wine glasses. Pour persimmon sauce over ice cream and serve immediately.

98 PINEAPPLE CREAM GATEAU

Serves
12 to 14

Preparation
25 minutes

Chill
3–24 hours

A very simple, but elegant, light dessert that is even better the next day. The recipe was given to *Private Collection* by a friend who brought it to us from her sojourn in Paris.

    5 ounces slivered almonds (use *only* slivered, not
       whole)
    1 16-ounce can pineapple slices*
    ¼ cup unsalted butter, softened
    ½ cup sugar
    4 egg yolks
    1 cup heavy cream
    2 teaspoons rum
    3 packages ladyfingers
    1½ cups heavy cream

Pulverize almonds in food processor or blender until *very* fine. Drain pineapple *well*, reserving juice, and finely chop. *(Do not substitute canned crushed pineapple. It is not of the same quality.)

In a mixing bowl, cream together butter and sugar. Add egg yolks, one at a time. Whip 1 cup cream until soft mounds form, and add to butter mixture. Add almonds, pineapple, and rum. Combine gently but thoroughly.

Oil a 10-inch, springform pan. Place a layer of ladyfingers (1 package) in bottom and drizzle with ⅓ of reserved pineapple juice. Spread with half of almond mixture, then another layer of ladyfingers. Drizzle with more pineapple juice. Repeat almond and ladyfinger layers, drizzling with last of juice. Cover and refrigerate several hours or overnight.

Within a few hours of serving time, remove outside of springform except bottom. Whip 1½ cups heavy cream until stiff and spread over all of dessert. Refrigerate.

Remove to a cake stand or serving platter and surround with dainty flowers or mint sprigs.

"It became increasingly difficult to find an appropriate gift for Papa, so one holiday I treated him to this wonderful almond torte. It's been his special Christmas present ever since."

Serves 12

Preparation
15 minutes

Baking
1 hour

1½ cups flour
5 tablespoons sugar
½ cup butter, softened
1 egg yolk, lightly beaten

Preheat oven to 325°. In a medium-sized bowl, combine flour and sugar. Using a pastry blender or 2 table knives, cut in butter until evenly mixed. Stir in egg yolk. (Do not be concerned about crumbly appearance.) Using your fingers, press pastry mixture into a fluted, 10-inch tart pan with a removable bottom, working it evenly over bottom and up sides.

8 ounces almond paste, crumbled
2 tablespoons sugar
2 tablespoons flour
2 eggs
1 egg white
½ teaspoon almond extract

Place almond paste, sugar, flour, and 2 eggs in an electric blender or food processor. Blend until smooth. Add egg white and almond extract. Blend again, then pour into pastry shell. Bake 1 hour or until top is a rich, golden brown. Cool 10 minutes before glazing.

½ cup sliced almonds
1 cup powdered sugar
2 tablespoons milk

While torte is cooling, spread almonds out on an ungreased cookie sheet and toast in oven at 325° for 10 minutes, until lightly browned. Combine powdered sugar and milk and spread over top of torte. Sprinkle with almonds. When cool, remove from pan and serve in small slices.

Note: This keeps beautifully!

100 SWEDISH RUM PUDDING

Serves
6 to 8

Preparation
30 minutes

Chill
2–3 hours

An old family recipe from Sweden that is light and lovely any time of the year . . . at summer dinner parties, surrounded with plump, fresh berries, or in a heart-shaped mold to celebrate St. Valentine's Day. BLUEBERRY KIR SAUCE would stand-in beautifully if raspberries aren't at hand.

> 1 packet unflavored gelatin
> ¾ cup sugar
> ¼ cup cold water
> 2 cups hot milk
> 5 egg yolks, lightly beaten
> ½ cup light rum
> 1 cup heavy cream

For a successful preparation, have the first 5 ingredients ready to go!

Combine gelatin and sugar in top of double boiler. With a whisk, add cold water then hot milk. Place over boiling water, continuing to beat with a whisk as you add the egg yolks. Beat until frothy and consistency of heavy cream; about 3–4 minutes. Cool, stirring periodically. (If you wish, set over a bowl of ice and stir with a whisk until room temperature.)

When mixture is cool, whisk in rum. Whip cream to the consistency of a thick pudding or mousse. Whisk cream into cooled mixture and pour into a well-oiled, 6-cup ring mold. Chill until set.

RASPBERRY SAUCE

> 1 10-ounce package frozen raspberries, thawed
> ¾ cup currant jelly
> 1 tablespoon cornstarch
> 1 tablespoon cold water
> 1 tablespoon Grand Marnier

Strain thawed berries through a sieve to attain ¾ cup juice. Combine juice and jelly in a small saucepan. Bring to a boil. Combine cornstarch and water and add to syrup. Stir constantly with a whisk until sauce is clear and thick. Remove from heat and stir in Grand Marnier. Cool.

This dessert looks so pretty served on a platter wreathed with mint leaves. Place a small bowl of the sauce in the center.

MOLASSES CRISPS 101

These are like lace cookies but quite easy to handle and certainly delicious! The dough keeps well in refrigerator or freezer for last-minute treats.

Yield
8 dozen

Preparation
15 minutes

Chill

Baking
8–10 minutes

¾ cup oatmeal
¾ cup sifted flour
1 cup sugar
½ teaspoon baking powder
¼ teaspoon salt
1 teaspoon cinnamon
¼ teaspoon ground cloves
½ cup butter, melted
¼ cup milk
¼ cup light molasses

Preheat oven to 350°. Combine dry ingredients and spices. Combine melted butter, milk, and molasses. Stir into dry ingredients until smooth. Chill for easier handling.

Oil foil-lined cookie sheets. Drop batter by ½-teaspoonfuls, 3–4 inches apart (9 per sheet). Bake 8–10 minutes. Let cool a half-minute before removing with a spatula.

102 CHESTNUT ROLL

Serves
12 to 14

Preparation
1 hour

Baking
12 minutes

A glorious, winter dessert that keeps beautifully. Dress it up for the holidays with sprigs of holly.

> ¾ cup sifted cake flour
> 1 teaspoon baking powder
> ¼ teaspoon salt
> 4 eggs
> ¾ cup sugar
> 1 teaspoon vanilla
> Powdered sugar

Preheat oven to 400°.

Line the bottom of a jelly roll pan (15 x 10 x 1 inches) with waxed paper to fit. Butter paper and sides of pan.

Sift flour, baking powder, and salt together. Beat the eggs until light and foamy. Continue beating, adding sugar gradually, until very pale and thick, and double in volume. (This will take 5–10 minutes, depending on power of electric mixer.) Beat in vanilla. Sprinkle dry ingredients over batter and fold in gently.

Pour batter into prepared pan and bake 12 minutes or until cake is delicately browned and top springs back to touch. Be careful not to overbake.

Spread a clean dish towel out on counter and sift powdered sugar evenly over surface. While cake is still warm, loosen around edges with a knife and turn out onto towel. Working quickly, carefully remove paper. Cut off crisp edges with a knife. Starting with *longer* edge, roll up cake, including the towel as you go so that cake will not stick to itself. Place wrapped cake on rack to cool.

CHESTNUT BUTTER CREAM

10–12 ounces of marrons in syrup, drained
    (or marrons glace)*
½ cup sugar
⅓ cup light corn syrup
3 egg yolks
½ pound unsalted butter, cut in pieces and
    softened
¼ cup dark rum

Shavings of bitter chocolate

Finely chop marrons. Combine sugar and corn syrup in a small saucepan. Cook over medium heat, stirring constantly, until it comes to a full boil. Remove from heat.

In a medium-sized bowl, beat eggs until lemon-colored. Gradually beat in hot syrup, continuing to beat until mixture is cool. Beat in butter, a piece at a time. Stir in rum and chestnuts.

Unroll cooled cake, removing towel. Spread top with half of butter cream. Reroll cake and place on serving platter. Frost with rest of butter cream. Decorate with chocolate shavings.

This may be prepared the day before and refrigerated.

*Note: Marrons (candied chestnuts) are readily available in specialty stores and many supermarkets.

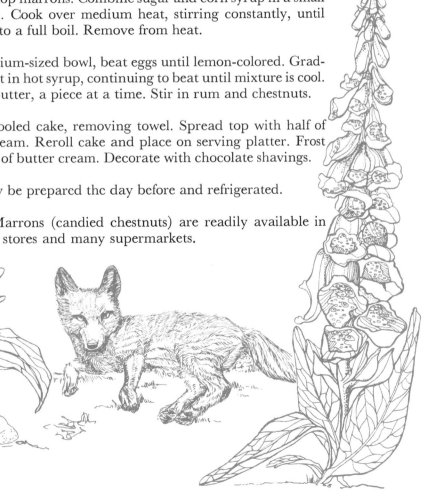

103 CHOCOLATE MOCHA BLITZ TORTE

Serves
8 to 10

Preparation
30 minutes

Baking
35 minutes

Cool

Our first *Private Collection* was dedicated to Aunt Bea and Aunt Jane, who symbolize those dear persons that each of us who loves to cook feels were and are our inspirations. In this collection, it seems most fitting to include a special recipe from each of their treasured files. This is Aunt Bea's superb dessert. Be sure to try Aunt Jane's CHOCOLATE SNOWBALLS.

2 ounces German sweet chocolate
¼ cup boiling water
½ cup butter, softened
1 cup sugar
2 egg yolks
1 teaspoon vanilla
1¼ cups sifted cake flour
¼ teaspoon salt
½ teaspoon baking soda
½ cup buttermilk
2 egg whites, stiffly beaten

Preheat oven to 325°. Melt chocolate in boiling water and cool. Grease and flour two 9 or 10-inch cake pans with removable bottoms.

In large mixing bowl, cream butter and sugar. Add egg yolks, one at a time, beating well. Add cooled chocolate and vanilla. Sift together flour, salt, and baking soda. Add to butter mixture, alternating with buttermilk. Blend well with each addition but do not overbeat. Fold in beaten egg whites. Divide batter between cake pans.

3 egg whites
¾ cup sugar
1 cup slivered almonds

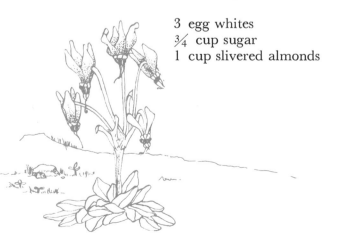

Beat egg whites until they form soft mounds. Gradually beat in sugar. When stiff peaks form, spread meringue over batter. Sprinkle with almonds. Bake 35–40 minutes, until an inserted toothpick tests clean. Cool completely on racks before removing from pans.

> 1 cup heavy cream
> 1 teaspoon instant coffee granules
> ¼ cup powdered sugar

Whip cream, adding coffee granules and powdered sugar. Spread between cooled layers and refrigerate until serving.

Note: The cake/meringue layers may be made a day ahead; also, they freeze beautifully.

CHOCOLATE SNOWBALLS 104

. . . dainty cookies to grace a tea table or holiday tray.

Yield
4 dozen

Preparation
15 minutes

Baking
15 minutes

> 1 cup butter, softened
> ⅔ cup powdered sugar
> 2 tablespoons cocoa
> 1½ cups sifted flour
> 1 teaspoon vanilla
> ½ cup chopped nuts (optional)
> Powdered sugar

Preheat oven to 350°.

With an electric beater, cream together butter, sugar, and cocoa. Beat in flour, then vanilla and nuts. Form into 1-inch balls (the dough will be rather soft), and bake on ungreased cookie sheets for 15 minutes. Sift powdered sugar over cookies when cool.

105 CLARA'S CHOCOLATE STEAMED PUDDING

Serves 6

Preparation
15 minutes

Steaming
2 hours

We know that this dates back to 1907, and probably many years before then. It's a marvelous winter dessert and may be made well in advance, and in larger quantities.

3 egg yolks
1 cup sugar
2 ounces unsweetened chocolate, melted
3 tablespoons milk
1 cup sifted flour
2 teaspoons baking powder
⅛ teaspoon salt
3 egg whites

In a mixing bowl, beat egg yolks until light. Gradually beat in sugar, then chocolate and milk. Sift together dry ingredients and stir into chocolate mixture with a rubber spatula. Beat egg whites until stiff but not dry. Fold into batter until thoroughly blended. Pour into a well-oiled, 1-quart, pudding mold and cover tightly with a lid or foil.

Use a kettle or roasting pan that is deeper than the mold. Place a rack in bottom to support mold, and fill with enough warm water not to evaporate during steaming; usually about 2 inches. Cover kettle tightly and steam on top of stove, or in uncovered roasting pan in 325° oven, for 2 hours, letting water just simmer.

While still warm, unmold pudding. Serve with the following sauce or FOAMY HARD SAUCE from our first *Private Collection*.

SAUCE

½ cup butter, softened
1 cup sugar
1 egg
½ teaspoon vanilla
¼ cup boiling water

In top of a double boiler, cream together butter and sugar. Beat in egg and vanilla, then boiling water. Keep hot over simmering water, but do not boil. Whisk just before serving. (If using a food processor, combine first 4 ingredients and, while processing, pour boiling water through tube. Before serving, heat in a double boiler.)

Note: The pudding may be made several days in advance and kept tightly sealed in refrigerator. Just re-steam, as directed, until heated through.

CHOCOLATE WAFERS 106

A vintage cookie to complement puddings, sherbets, ice cream . . .

Yield
5 dozen

Preparation
15 minutes

Baking
10 minutes

½ cup butter, softened
1 cup sugar
2 ounces unsweetened chocolate, melted
1 egg, well-beaten
2 tablespoons milk
2¼ cups sifted flour
1 teaspoon cinnamon (optional)
½ teaspoon baking soda
¼ teaspoon salt

Preheat oven to 350°. Cream together butter and sugar. Beat in chocolate, then egg and milk. Sift together dry ingredients and stir into batter. Roll dough out to ⅛-inch thickness and cut into rounds or special shapes. Bake 10 minutes.

This dough is ideal for a cookie press or can be formed into a roll and frozen, then sliced for quick treats.

107 HAZELNUT CREAM CAKE

Serves 14

Preparation
30 minutes
15 minutes

Cooling

Baking
20 minutes

A lovely cake for a christening or elegant luncheon, one of its many virtues is that it is better made a day or two ahead. As a dramatic dessert for a crowd, it may be doubled yet still assembled as one cake.

> 6 tablespoons butter, melted and cooled
> 1 cup sugar
> 6 eggs, separated
> 1 tablespoon vanilla
> ¼ teaspoon cream of tartar
> 3 tablespoons sugar
> 1½ cups sifted cake flour
> ¾ cup hazelnuts, toasted and finely chopped
> (see index)

Preheat oven to 350°. Butter bottoms and sides of 3 9-inch cake pans and line each with circles of wax paper. Butter paper. Melt 6 tablespoons butter, and set aside to cool.

In a large mixing bowl, combine 1 cup sugar, egg yolks, and vanilla. With an electric mixer, beat until thick and *very* pale yellow; about 5 minutes. Beat egg whites with cream of tartar until soft peaks form. Gradually beat in 3 tablespoons sugar. Continue beating until stiff peaks form.

Fold ¼ of egg whites into egg yolk mixture, then alternate portions of flour (sifting over batter) and egg whites, folding after each addition. Toward end of folding process, add cooled butter in 2 stages, leaving milky residue in bottom of saucepan. Gently fold in hazelnuts, but don't overmix or you will lose volume.

Divide batter between pans, but do not be concerned about small amount. Bake 20 minutes or until lightly browned and just beginning to shrink from sides of pans. Cool 10 minutes before inverting onto racks and removing papers.

Glaze each layer with the following syrup. (If doubling recipe, split the cakes to make 6 layers. While still warm, glaze *uncut* sides of layers with syrup).

½ cup sugar
3 tablespoons water
3 tablespoons Frangelico liqueur

Combine sugar and water in a saucepan. Simmer over low heat for 2 minutes without stirring. Cool and add Frangelico before brushing on cakes.

At this point, if cake is being made many days in advance, wrap layers in foil and freeze.

CREAM FILLING

2 teaspoons gelatin
3 tablespoons cold water
8 ounces cream cheese, softened to room temperature
⅓ cup powdered sugar
1 teaspoon vanilla extract
3 cups heavy cream
½ cup hazelnuts, toasted and finely chopped

In a small bowl, sprinkle gelatin over water to soften for 10 minutes. Set bowl over simmering water and stir to dissolve.

In a large mixing bowl, beat together cream cheese (it *must* be room temperature), warm gelatin, powdered sugar, and vanilla. Gradually beat in cream until soft peaks form.

To assemble, use ⅔ of cream filling to sandwich the 3 layers (6 layers, if recipe is being doubled). Frost sides and top with rest, and sprinkle with hazelnuts. Refrigerate until ready to serve (up to 2 days). Serve in thin slices.

108 BREAD PUDDING with APPLES

Serves 8

*Preparation
25 minutes*

*Baking
1½–2 hours*

If there are those who do not care for bread puddings, this may change their minds. The apples, lending special flavor and texture, make this an ideal fall dessert.

> 1½ pounds baking apples
> ¼ cup butter
> 2 tablespoons sugar
> ¼ teaspoon cinnamon
> 1 1-pound loaf French bread
> ¼ cup butter, softened
> ¼ cup seedless raisins
> 4 eggs
> 1 quart milk
> ⅔ cup sugar
> 2 teaspoons vanilla
> Grating of nutmeg
> Lightly whipped cream (optional)

Preheat oven to 325°.

Peel, core, and cut apples into large dice. Melt ¼ cup butter in a large, heavy skillet. Add apples, sprinkling with 2 tablespoons sugar and the cinnamon. Sauté over medium heat for about 10 minutes, stirring frequently.

Remove crusts from bread and cut into ½ to ¾-inch cubes. Liberally grease a deep, 2½-quart, baking dish with the remaining ¼ cup butter, then add what is left to the bread cubes, cutting into bits. Combine bread, raisins, apples, and the pan juices in the baking dish.

Combine eggs, milk, sugar, vanilla, and nutmeg, beating lightly with a whisk. Pour over bread and apples.

Set dish in a shallow pan filled with 1-inch warm water. Bake for 1½ hours or until set. (This may take 2 hours, depending on type of casserole.) Serve hot with lightly whipped cream.

This is truly an old, family recipe, and every bit as good as it sounds. A subtly flavored spice cake, its marvelous height and unusual colors make a dramatic showing at any table.

Serves
14 to 18

Preparation
25 minutes

Baking
30 minutes

1 cup butter, softened
2 cups sugar
4 eggs, separated*
1 cup seedless blackberry jam
3 cups sifted flour
½ teaspoon ground cloves
½ teaspoon nutmeg
1 teaspoon cinnamon
1 teaspoon baking soda
1 cup buttermilk
1 cup pecans or walnuts, chopped (optional)
½ teaspoon salt

*Note: Your cake will be particularly successful if you have the eggs at room temperature. To achieve this quickly, place them in hot water for several minutes (Don't worry! They won't crack.) while preparing cake pans and creaming butter and sugar.

Preheat oven to 325°. Butter and flour 3 9-inch cake pans. Cream together butter and sugar. Beat in egg yolks, one at a time, then blackberry jam. Resift flour with spices and baking soda. Add to butter mixture in 3 parts, alternating with buttermilk. Blend thoroughly each time but do not over-beat. Fold in nuts.

Beat egg whites with salt until stiff but not dry. Gently fold into batter. Pour into prepared pans.

Bake for 30–35 minutes, just until cakes begin to loosen at edges. Completely cool in pans before removing, then spread with HONEY ICING.

110 HONEY ICING

Preparation
15 minutes

A satiny, old-fashioned icing for spice cakes.

> 1 16-ounce jar light-colored honey
> 3 egg whites
> ⅛ teaspoon salt
> ¼ teaspoon almond extract
> ¼ teaspoon vanilla

In a medium saucepan over medium-high heat, boil honey, without stirring, for about 10 minutes; until it reaches thread stage (about 252°). Beat egg whites with salt until stiff but not dry. Continuing to beat, pour honey into egg whites in a thin stream. Add almond and vanilla flavorings.

Spread between layers and on top and sides of cake, creating pretty swirls and peaks. Surround cake with whole strawberries or seasonal flowers for a special touch.

111 CREAM CHEESE NUT COOKIES

Yield
3 dozen

Preparation
20 minutes

Chill

Baking
10 minutes

A special cookie for special occasions.

> 1 cup sifted flour
> ½ cup butter, softened
> 3 ounces cream cheese, softened
> ⅓ cup chopped nuts
> 2 tablespoons sugar
> ¼ teaspoon vanilla
> Powdered sugar

Preheat oven to 400°. Combine flour, butter, and cream cheese. Chill. Roll out to ⅛-inch thickness. Cut into circles (about 2½ inches).

Combine remaining ingredients. Place a teaspoon or so of nut mixture on each circle of dough. Fold over, pressing edges with a fork to seal. Bake 10 minutes on ungreased cookie sheets. While hot, roll in powdered sugar.

CONTRIBUTORS

League Members

Terry Maull Akerman
Alice Charleston Anderson
Mary McIlrath Baumel
Margaret Rossotti Beltramo
Cheryl Roudabush Benedict
Jennifer Better
Pamela Flebbe Brandin
Joan Beaumont Brown
Pamela Winters Brown
Julie Bachman-Stearns Burian
Carolyn Fulgham Butcher
Lindsay Hafer Carpenter
Susan Lecocq Coan
Gretchen Snyder Conlan
Bunny Rankin Davis
Kristine Schray Erving
Janet Hartwell Eyre
Marcia Grant French
Carol Connelly Friedman
Patricia Ireland Fuller
Ginger Alfs Glockner
Mary Schutte Gullixson
Joan Emery Hagey
Betsy Lovell Hawley
Judith Rockwell Humphreys
Ann Christian Kalar
Nancy Hunt Kiesling
Kristin Ekstrom Klint
Kathryn Mitchell Ladra
Mary Liz Hufnagel Maletis

Lynn Hochschwender McGowin
Mimi Platt Menard
Sharon Zweig Meresman
Bonnie Stewart Mickelson
Carole Pfetcher Montgomery
Anne Wright Murphy
Elizabeth Strand Nyberg
Phoebe Allen Olcott
Doris Montara Passalacqua
Judith Gillfillan Pence
Mary Halstead Pickard
Patricia Rae Pipkin
Dianne Johnson Pitts
Betsy Rabbitt Pomeroy
Marilyn Moore Pratt
Linda Lowry Romley
Karen Strandhagen Ross
Lisa Longaker Ross
Catherine Kinney Salera
Sonia Wakefield Shepard
Donna Richards Sheridan
Jamie Bingham Sidells
Lisa Page Simon
Virginia Michael Sproul
Jane Warnke Stocklin
Mary Davis Sweeney
Christine Larson Terborgh
Shirley Brennan Turner
Vivien Stephen Webb
Carol Haley Welsh

League Friends

Peggy Giesey Ashby
Joyce Cuneo Castellino
Kay Alexander Clark
Margaret Cutshall
Dorothy Dike
Martha Martz Grant
Simonne O'Grady Greene
Marcy Aylward Harris

Gloria and Charles Maita
Christy Williams Oster
Nancy Sievers Schmoll
Clara Smith Spalding
Dorothy Unger Telfer
Katherine Martin Wagner
Pam McIlwaine Yaeger
Dalva Galeno Youngblood

Special Recognition

Lois McCubbin Burrows
Charlotte Combe
Linda Diener Grant

Lou Seibert Pappas
Kim Bacon Peterson
Diana and Paul Welanetz

ADDENDUM

PHYLLO (also known as fila, filo, fillo, or streudel leaves) can be found in 1-pound packages in the freezer or deli sections of most markets. If frozen, thaw according to package instructions. It is vital that the phyllo not dry out, so do not unwrap package until all of your recipe ingredients have been assembled. Keep a damp towel over the strips that you'll be using, removing only 1 at a time and working quickly.

THE ARTIST

Once more, Linda Newberry has touched the pages with her exceptional drawings of plant and wildlife in northern California. A native Californian, she was founder of Deer Hollow Farm on the San Antonio Open Space Preserve in Los Altos, California. She is an environmental educator, using her perceptive art skills to enhance her teaching. Presently, she resides in Cannon Beach, on the far north coast of Oregon.

All of the plants and animals that she has represented in this book are to be found in our woods, meadows, bogs, and marshes in the springtime. It is a delight to hunt for the striped skunk, house wren, lupine, bumblebee, Douglas iris, blue-eyed grass, blue dicks, wood violets, sticky monkey flower, blue-eyed Mary, dark-eyed junco, fivespot, fritillary butterfly, baby-blue-eyes, beaver, water ouzel (dipper), cattails, stream orchid, horsetail, skunk cabbage, California pitcher plant (cobra plant blossom), corn lily, coltsfoot, false Solomon's seal, wood fern, clintonia, yellow pond lily, fiddleneck, wild strawberry, fox pup, shooting stars, tiger lily, trillium, foxglove, calypso orchid, brush rabbit, Matilija poppy, Chinese houses, California poppies, monkshood, sweet woodruff, pussy willows, Ithuriel's spear, tulips, owl's clover, baby thrushes, wood sorrel, robin, Anna's hummer, fire-cracker flower, globe lily, mariposa lily, miner's lettuce, phlox, farewell-to-spring, wild currant (red-flowering), sun cups, mule ears, tree frog, damselfly, and cricket.

THE DESIGNER

Gerald W. Stratford is a fourth-generation Californian whose family has contributed to the Bay Area tradition of fine typography, printing and book binding since 1906. The Stratford Colophon symbolically recalls the phoenix to commemorate the growth of this tradition from the ashes of San Francisco's great fire. Mr. Stratford currently heads STRATFORD DESIGN ASSOCIATES, *a full-service group of illustrators, calligraphers and designers specializing in corporate identity and trademark development. The Stratford atelier in Brisbane, though just minutes from downtown San Francisco on the north slope of San Bruno mountain, is surrounded by one of the greatest profusions of wildflowers in California.*

This book was elegantly set with great care and love by the journeymen of the Mackenzie-Harris chapel in San Francisco.

The proceeds from the sale of this book will be returned to the community through projects sponsored by the Junior League of Palo Alto, Inc.